THE SIZE
OF GOD

THE SIZE
OF GOD

The Theology
of Bernard Loomer in Context

edited by

William Dean and *Larry E. Axel*

Mercer
University Press

The paper used in this publication meets
the minimum requirements of American National Standard
for Information Sciences—Permanence of Paper
for Printed Library Materials, ANSI Z39.48-1984.

Library of Congress Cataloging-in-Publication Data
The Size of God.

Published also as v. 8, nos. 1 & 2 of the American jour-
nal of theology & philosophy.
"Published works by Bernard M. Loomer": p. 18
1. God—History of doctrines—20th century.
2. Process theology—History.   3. Loomer, Bernard.
I. Loomer, Bernard.   II. Dean, William D.   III. Axel,
Larry E., 1946-
BT102.L58S58   1987   231   86-31250
ISBN 0-86554-255-4 (alk. paper)

CONTENTS

PREFACE

Bernard Loomer's "The Size of God" is a distinct option in process theology and in empirical theology. Further, it advances neglected theories not only about religious identity, but about the American character.

Loomer here proposes that empirical religious thought must never in any way be detached from natural and social history; it must reach all the way to the limits of natural and social history. Religious thought must be historical thought, but it must also identify God with the whole of the natural and social world. The effort to identify God with a part, rather than the whole, of the natural world is empirically unwarranted, even if it protects the divine virtue by associating God with only the goodness of the world. To relate God to only a part is to identify God with abstractions—abstractions away from concrete natural experience, abstractions exercised by virtually all American religious naturalists.

At the same time Loomer sharpens that distinct image of the American introduced by William James, John Dewey, and William Carlos Williams. In contrast to both the innocent American rustic and the other-worldly American pilgrim, Loomer's "earth-creature" has a sense of the tragic and a commitment to the concrete. For this character, whose "spirit had its origin in the flames of the stars and the dust of the planet," there is ambiguity in all areas of the world, even in God.

"The Size of God" has had three major public hearings: in 1977 at the Graduate Theological Union, in 1978 at a special session of the national meeting of the American Academy of Religion, and in 1979 at a second special session of the national meeting of the American Academy of Religion. Both American Academy of Religion sessions were initiated and organized by Bernard Lee. In the 1978 session the formal respondents were Lewis Ford and Nancy Frankenberry; in the 1979 session the formal respondents were John Cobb, Jr., Delwin Brown, and William Dean. These public meetings were controversial, a condition stimulated not only by the distinctiveness of Loomer's argument but by the way his prose leans into the wind.

John Cobb's and Delwin Brown's responses are reprinted here in virtually the same form they were originally written. Bernard Lee and Larry Axel offer new responses. William Dean and Nancy Frankenberry have relinquished their original responses in order to frame this discussion—Dean initially to summarize and amplify a few developments in Loomer's life and thought that appear to anticipate his last major writing, and Frankenberry finally to bring Loomer's orientation into conversation with the four responses.

Bernard Loomer died on 15 August 1985, as some of us still worked toward the completion of these pages.

INTRODUCTION: FROM INTEGRITY TO SIZE

William Dean / Gustavus Adolphus College

Bernard Loomer's father was a sea captain. He was acquainted with his small place in an uncontrollable nature. In a talk in 1974 Loomer described his father's instructions about the uses of a baseball glove. The father had just overheard his son's sandlot complaints about the thinness of a glove inherited from his older brothers. When his father asked him what a baseball glove was for, young Loomer had said that it was to protect the hand. In the words of Bernard Loomer in his sixties, his father replied:

> Son, I never have played baseball, but it seems to me you ought to be able to catch the ball bare-handed. The way I look at it, you use a glove not to protect your hand, but to give you a bigger hand to help catch balls that are more difficult to reach. I assume that in this as in all walks of life there are tricks to the trade. I suggest you learn how to catch with that glove for two reasons. First, because you are not going to get another one, and second, because you don't need protection from life. You need a glove to give you a bigger hand to catch baseballs you might otherwise miss.[1]

As the decade of the 1970s progressed, Loomer reflected increasingly on the fact that what you might otherwise miss was irrational, even evil, but must be caught anyway. Loomer grew increasingly dissatisfied with those who seemed to restrict their reach—even Whitehead was faulted. And, increasingly, it appeared that Christian theology was the theology Loomer had—that he was not going to get another one—and so, although it was thin in places, he attempted to use the one theology he had, to catch all he could.

Loomer's story about his father suggests the meaning of Loomer's special term, "size," or of its synonym, "stature." Size signifies "the volume of life you can take into your being and still maintain your integrity."[2] Both size and integrity were important in Loomer's own lexicon; but size arose later and by 1974 supplanted integ-

---

[1]Bernard M. Loomer, "Remarks by Bernard M. Loomer," *Alumni* (published by the Divinity School of the University of Chicago, October 1974): 4.

[2]Bernard M. Loomer, "S-I-Z-E," *Criterion* 13 (Spring 1974): 6.

rity and became Loomer's "word," in which integrity served as only a factor.[3] From the preceding three decades the balance had shifted; the rationalism of integrity became only a limit on the now central aestheticism and empiricism of size, or stature.

At the end of the decade, after writing "The Size of God," Loomer would say:

> I wish the essential cast of my thought had matured earlier in my life. I need another 20 years to work it out. . . . The Size of God article is wide open to all sorts of attacks. It is so incomplete. It is in some respects an interim report. It lacks adequate development, especially with respect to the religious consequences of the position. Also I need to spell out the ontology of ambiguity. It will take a while to get accustomed to a God who lacks unambiguous perfection (a redundancy). For most people this kind of a God is nonsense. It not only lacks necessity; it lacks perfection. So from Hartshorne's point of view it is doubly cursed.[4]

I The Anticipations

The importance of accepting what you had was presented sharply to Loomer when in 1945, at the age of thirty-three, he was asked to be dean of the Divinity School. He followed the mature Ernest Cadman Caldwell, who went on to become president of the University of Chicago. Preceding Caldwell, he was asked to follow the two leading scholars of the "Chicago School" of theology: Shirley Jackson Case and Shailer Mathews. Case had capped a venerable career as New Testament scholar and as church historian with the deanship (1933-1938); and Shailer Mathews, while dean (1908-1933), became the nation's leading modernist religious scholar. Loomer had barely completed his dissertation. He asked to meet with Chancellor Robert Maynard Hutchins to discuss the idea of his appointment. After expatiating on the impropriety of asking a youth to take such an assignment, the assistant professor asked the chancellor, "Do I understand your silence correctly, namely, that as far as you are concerned I don't have much choice in the matter?" The chancellor responded, "That's about the size of it."[5] Of course, there was a choice, but it was framed within limits: take it too young or abandon the opportunity.

Loomer remained dean until 1953, but his career was awkwardly reversed: first he assumed the institutional leadership granted his predecessors only after they had attained scholarly eminence; then, fifteen years into his academic career, he tried to give his reading and writing the time they had deserved earlier. His deanship was and still is criticized for its rough unorthodoxy, and his early and hurried writing was and still is criticized for its youthful dogmatism, its Whiteheadian orthodoxy. Neverthe-

---

[3]"Last night at a little informal dinner Chuck Long asked me what I am calling it now. This question is not original with Mr. Long, but he is the one perhaps that has capitalized on it more than any other member of the faculty—since he knows what I used to call it. And I replied, and that is what I want to talk about: 'Today I call it S-I-Z-E' " (ibid., 5). I assume, perhaps incorrectly, that "integrity" is what he used to call it.

[4]A letter from Bernard M. Loomer to the author, 8 October 1979.

[5]Loomer, "Remarks," 2.

less, both these early careers were remarkable for their impact, particularly because they came from a such young man in theology, which was then such an old man's game.

The image of integrity was the preoccupation of these earlier years of Loomer's work, both as an original "process theologian" and as dean. As a Whitehead scholar he had stressed (and even this word is too weak) the integralness of Alfred North Whitehead's metaphysics (the "categoreal scheme" of *Process and Reality*) to suggest how twentieth-century theology might be made integral. As dean he argued for the integralness of the institution's life to suggest how students' lives might be made integral. Although he spoke of experience and of empiricism, his concerns were rationalistic in nature: they were dominated more by the ideal of order than by anything else.

Now anything but a rationalistic orientation is suggested by the title of Loomer's 1942 University of Chicago dissertation: "The Theological Significance of the Method of Empirical Analysis in the Philosophy of A. N. Whitehead." As the discussion in process thought subsequently developed, two camps were formed, the empirical and the rational.[6] It came to seem that if Loomer titled his dissertation "empirical analysis," he opposed the primacy of rational analysis. But, of course, it is anachronistic to say that the 1942 choice to use the word *empirical* was a decision against an as-yet-unformed rationalistic camp of process theologians.

In fact, Loomer's dissertation is rationalistic. Admittedly, Loomer was not an a priori rationalist. He was an empiricist to the extent that he could say that if there is no empirical warrant for an idea, then the idea is unacceptable; for example, because there is no empirical warrant for affirming the "everlastingness" of Whitehead's God, Loomer was unwilling to endorse the idea.[7] Further, Loomer's instinct, unlike that of a Charles Hartshorne, was not to use "necessary" characteristics of reasoning in the effort to establish what was "necessarily" true about God. Nevertheless, rationalism, in the sense of prizing the order of things over the concrete particularity of things, received Loomer's fervent support. Loomer was an empiricist primarily (if not only) in the sense that he framed the question about general conditions by asking what they must be "if we are to have any experience at all."[8] Loomer's actual analysis focused on two aspects of Whitehead's philosophy: First, the effort to characterize the most general structures of experience; and second, the effort to construct, using these general structures of experience, "a system of general ideas."[9] This was a "rationalism" in that it discussed general structures you could imagine and the systems into which you could place these structures. It followed, then, that for Loomer

---

[6]See, e.g., Bernard J. Lee, S.M., "Two Process Theologies," *Theological Studies* 45 (1984): 307-19.

[7]Bernard M. Loomer, "Whitehead's Method of Empirical Analysis," in *Process Theology: Basic Writings by the Key Thinkers of a Major Movement,* ed. Ewert H. Cousins (New York: Newman Press, 1971) 82. This writing is a selection from Loomer's dissertation.

[8]Ibid., 68.

[9]Ibid., 69.

God was proffered as a solution to the problem of why and how structures and systems in and about existence are possible.[10]

Loomer's defense of process theology tended to be a defense of rationalism. This was Loomer's approach in his 1949 "Christian Faith and Process Philosophy," in which he supported, against neo-orthodox critics, the use of process philosophy in Christian theology. "Rationalism," Loomer said, "in the widest sense, involves some kind of system; it emphasizes primarily continuity of explanation."[11] Rationalism is important because it offers clarity to the theologian about the presupposed and systematic world views necessary to every theology.

> The necessity of system or coherence is grounded in the intellectual and religious demand for integrity, for unity, for an undivided self. We cannot worship our sovereign Lord if we are divided and compartmentalized selves. Integrity both presupposes and brings about self-consciousness, that is, the awareness of who one is, where one stands and why he stands there, and what God one commits himself to. But we cannot be sufficiently self-conscious without having probed the depths of our cultural and religious presuppositions.[12]

It appears, then, that the key to religious faith is integrity and the key to integrity is consciousness about world views. Accordingly, Loomer argues that process philosophy's world view contributes to consciousness, integrity, and religious faith by providing a peculiarly contemporary set of metaphysical presuppositions. It will contribute to the theologian's effort to be more conscious of his or her world views, and to better evaluate those world views for their contemporary adequacy. (Loomer did qualify his rationalism, saying that faith precedes reason and that faith contributes to reason, just as reason contributes to faith. Not surprisingly, he concludes that "faith and reason are not synonymous."[13])

The same rationalistic emphasis on integralness is found in Loomer's philosophy of education and in his work as dean of the Divinity School. While serving as dean in 1951 Loomer wrote "Religion and the Mind of the University," which is both a diatribe against the academic preoccupation with "competency" and a call for academic "integrity." The university professor not only idolizes scholarly competency, but becomes virtually warped: "One great possible danger of concentrated and prolonged specialized discipline is the atrophy of a sensitive awareness to the fundamental and pervasive features of everyday life."[14] Competency, in short, disables one's capacity to see the rationalistic unities in life. A concern for integrity, Loomer argues, would revive that waning rationalistic dimension: "Intellectual integrity in-

---

[10]Ibid., 79-80.

[11]Bernard M. Loomer, "Christian Faith and Process Philosophy," *Process Philosophy and Christian Thought,* ed. Delwin Brown, Ralph E. James, and Gene Reeves (Indianapolis and New York: Bobbs-Merrill Company, Inc., 1971) 71.

[12]Ibid., 74.

[13]Ibid., 75.

[14]Bernard M. Loomer, "Religion and the Mind of the University," in *Liberal Learning and Religion,* ed. Amos N. Wilder (Port Washington NY: Kennikat Press, 1969) 156.

volves the idea of wholeness, of unity, wherein the several disciplines that make up a university are synthesized."[15] And why is an integral university valuable for the student? Because integrity in the university would give students a rational integrity. For the Divinity School the curricular consequences of Loomer's emphasis on integrity were manifold. Out of the period of Loomer's deanship came the "dialogical fields," such as "Theology and Literature," "Ethics and Society," and "Religion and Personality," which by their very self-definition pursued integrity. Out of this period came what was known as the "oral statement": a brief written statement by the student, indicating the more general meanings of the dissertation project and providing a focus for the Ph.D. oral examination. If there was an atmosphere Loomer hoped would pervade the Divinity School, it was based on the demand that each individual, both faculty and student, attain and demand his or her rational integrity.

As late as 1965, in a lecture given at the time of his departure from the University of Chicago to become professor of philosophical theology at the Graduate Theological Union in Berkeley, Loomer made the startling proposal—surely an affront to those who treasured disinterested research—that "all degrees are awarded on the basis of an achieved maturity."[16] Among the criteria for measuring and assessing maturity were two that pertained especially to the ideal of integrity. First, maturity is the capacity for intellectual love, and "intellectual love is a passion for truth." Second, maturity "is the capacity for systematic thought. Thought by its very nature deals with relations, and systematic thought is simply thinking carried through to its logical and natural conclusion. It is a concern for wholeness, unity, and coherence. It is a search for intellectual integrity, a reaching out for a unified vision of meaning, which is an essential component of personal integrity."[17]

Then, nine years later, Loomer's response to a paper given by David Griffin at a conference on process philosophy and biblical theology began by noting that Griffin's paper was "a very nice reminder to me of where I no longer stand." He went on to say, "Things have happened to me, in my thinking, that cause me to try to understand what Mr. Griffin is about and why he goes at it this way."[18] Griffin, Loomer said, had sought a conceptual basis for "the appropriate response to revelation," a conceptual basis telling us how to interpret revelation. Griffin (who in his own ways was to change in the coming years) had relied on conceptions that reside "too much in clear situations conceptually dealt with. That is, the appropriateness is finally, for me, too abstract and not related to the ambiguities of life and contexts."[19] Loomer, now calling on a somewhat different Whitehead, cited "the Whiteheadian axiom" that "when you're clear you know you're superficial." Stated technically, Loomer suggested that for God,

---

[15]Ibid., 162.

[16]Bernard M. Loomer, *Criterion* 4 (Autumn 1965): 4.

[17]Ibid., 4-5.

[18]Bernard M. Loomer, "Response to David R. Griffin," *Encounter* 36 (1975): 361.

[19]Ibid., 368.

there is no specific aim for any concrete individual. I used to think there was; and I thought the whole problem was that sometimes the concrete individual subjectively did not fully realize the initial aim that God had provided for that occasion. I see now that I was mistaken, and I have repented of the error of my ways. And if you say that my understanding is not Whiteheadian, and Whitehead is still back where I was, then I only have to say that Whitehead, I hope, is now repenting of the error of *his* ways![20]

If, in short, a Whiteheadian abandons hope that there is for any individual a specific and appropriate aim, then that Whiteheadian abandons the notion that the concrete is preceded by any specific, guiding ideal. And if the precession of the ideal is abandoned, then so is rationalism and so is the primacy of integrity—the belief that a general idea of one's own unity is the clue to how one should live.

The new Loomer now lectured that whatever is "the 'appropriate' does not get description"—that is, it is not learned through rational analysis but through empirical analysis. "There is no conceptual basis for normativeness beyond or independent of the efficient and persuasive power of the empirical and the historical. In this sense the actual is not the realization of a possible norm, conceptual or otherwise. The norm lies within the empirical, the historical itself."[21] Conceptual norms, rather, are mere abstractions from what is concrete. For example, the quest for the historical Jesus is "absolutely essential"; the notion of Jesus as "the realization of the logos" is simply an evasion of the only important point, that is the empirical, the historical. "In that sense I would understand Tillich to be one who likes his security with a passion. He doesn't want to be upset by historical inquiries."[22]

Loomer goes on to say, "I would understand the upset, and one does subject himself to the contingencies or whatever. But, I think, this is the nature of the primacy of the actual, the concrete, the historical." Even Whitehead in a Tillichian way fled the historical when he proposed a fundamental metaphysical distinction between the process of creativity and the primordial nature of God, the course of history and one aspect of God. "I think," said Loomer, that "this is fundamentally fatal in the long run" and process theology should reject it.[23] The truth about history is that in it the good and the evil are inextricably combined. When you regard the weakness and the evil in a person you look in exactly the same place that you look when you regard that person's strength and goodness—in *"exactly* the same place. Otherwise, if this were not so, you could transform an individual as it were by exorcising the distinguishable, separate evil elements within him. But you can't. When you do this you cut out his heart, you cut out his strength also."[24] "Concretely, I think we are faced with ambiguity on every side, at every moment." Then Loomer follows the threads of his own remarks: If God is to be known empirically, and not rationalistically, does the category of the ambiguous apply to God as well? "I hesitate to say that I want to

---

[20]Ibid., 364.

[21]Ibid., 363.

[22]Ibid.

[23]Ibid., 364.

[24]Ibid., 367.

have God responsible for evil, but sometimes I find myself moving this way, and perhaps even becoming more Jewish, or certain aspects of being Jewish, in thought. But at least tentatively I want to relate God and evil much more closely than I think Whitehead does."[25] On the issue of evil and God, not only is Loomer willing to distinguish himself from Whitehead, he is willing to assess Whitehead's motives. Whitehead's distinction between the realm of creativity and the primordial nature of God is designed, finally, "to relieve God of the responsibility for evil."[26] Loomer extends the analysis into motives in a way that must surely have offended his politically liberal colleagues in process theology at this conference in late February-early March 1974.

> If you will, at times I sense in Whitehead a desire to be too moral about keeping God clean. I say this because increasingly I come to understand that moral passion is a way of making problems manageable. You can work up a good sweat this way, because this is a way of taking an unmanageable problem and making it into a manageable problem; you can deal with it authentically. We can get all hot about Watergate, as though the issue were corruption. Aesthetically, the trouble was that you had a small guy living in a large house trying to do an impossible job with one cylinder. And you can't impeach him upon constitutional grounds if he makes a constitutional mistake; and this, I take it, is why we're morally concerned about this—in order to get him out, because we can't get him out otherwise.[27]

The issue, said Loomer, is power. Political power, in particular, is raw and ambiguous, and such power is better approached through an empiricism capable of dealing with what is raw and ambiguous. In his own way Loomer is proposing a radical empiricism, which acknowledges that what is raw and ambiguous must be approached through a largely inarticulate, bodily sensibility, rather than through the clarity of the five senses. Power at the deepest and most confusing level must be sensed primarily as an aesthetic phenomenon and analyzed aesthetically, rather than sensed primarily as a rational or moral phenomenon, and analyzed rationalistically or morally. The aesthetic, it appears to Loomer, is "that form of order which can most appropriately deal with the tensions involved in deep ambiguities."[28]

This is a reading of Loomer's ruminations in 1974, which in published form appear so rough, stumbling, and spontaneously colorful that they must be a transcription of seemingly off-the-cuff set of remarks. They show Loomer letting go of rationalism and the primacy of integrity, and moving in the direction of empiricism. The irreducibly ambiguous character of the empirically known world leaves the observer with irreducible tensions between weakness and strength, between good and evil, between a god of goodness and a god of evil. This ambiguity cannot be managed; rational and moral categories will not comprehend it. Hence, there is the suggestion that only aesthetics provides a way to organize radically empirical phenomena.

---

[25]Ibid., 366.

[26]Ibid.

[27]Ibid., 367.

[28]Ibid., 368.

By no means, however, is this to imply that by 1974 Loomer had simply turned the corner. In a lecture entitled "Theology and the Arts," given in March 1974 closely following his response to David Griffin, he returns to the aesthetic. Unlike, he says, the rational, the moral, or other conventional senses of the religious, the aesthetic sense of the religious is adequate as "a generalization of the value principle involved in the notion of evolutionary advance." It is "more dynamically historical as a type of order than these other types of order." However, the real thrust of the lecture is a splenetic complaint that artists fail to generalize their findings: "Those who can conceptualize their understanding, teach, and those who cannot, perform." The lecture turns back to the ideal of integrity and attempts to domesticate the aesthetic in its terms.

Four years later the aesthetic appears again in the lists of Loomer's efforts. In February 1978 he lectured at the Minneapolis College of Art and Design, and then again at the University of Montana on aesthetics and social practice. The lectures were taken from a forty-six-page document that Loomer entitled, "Notes on Beauty as a Design for Life." Loomer introduces his "Notes" by saying, "The lecture constitutes a reiterated suggestion that process-relational philosophy must become a mode of life and not just a mode of thought."[29] Near the end of the "Notes" Loomer cites the accepted distinction between the rationalistic, lineal, grammatical left hemisphere and the artistic, mystery-tolerant right hemisphere. Then he says, "I, who have been reared and educated in terms of the left hemisphere, find myself moving toward the right in order to achieve more of a balance."[30] Loomer goes on to claim Whitehead as balanced, but adds not without a grimace (one trusts) at his former self: "What I dislike in so many Whiteheadians is a loss of this balance and a great emphasis on the left hemisphere, the logical side of things."[31]

The problem addressed by the "Notes" is the character of American and, increasingly, of Western (if not of world) culture. Writing from the West Coast, thirteen years out of the University of Chicago, forty years after confronting Shirley Jackson Case and the last years of the "sociohistorical method" of the Chicago School of theology, Loomer adopted as his primary referent the social history of the American people. Both Case and Shailer Mathews had analyzed the figures and writings of the Bible and of church history exclusively in their social context; then, pursuing the second step of the sociohistorical method, they had evaluated those same figures and writings by examining them in the social context of twentieth-century America, using an implicitly pragmatic criterion. Case, Mathews, Gerald Birney Smith, and other proponents of the sociohistorical method in the first five decades of the century had rejected the isolation and absolutization of the text implicit in literary approaches to the Bible,[32] of the rational idea implicit in epistemological idealism, and of the

---

[29]Bernard M. Loomer, "Notes on Beauty as a Design for Life," a lecture at the Minneapolis College of Art and Design and at the University of Montana (1978), introductory page.

[30]Ibid., 37.

[31]Ibid., 38.

[32]Robert W. Funk, "The Watershed of the American Biblical Tradition: The Chicago School, First Phase, 1892-1920," *Journal of Biblical Literature* 95 (1976): 4-22.

scientific law implicit in positivism.[33] They treated religion as a social reality, not as a textual, ideational, or natural-scientific reality. Religion was something people used to enhance their present social existence, not something they used to replicate the dogmas of earlier peoples. Loomer, after decades spent exhorting others to see clearly the rational order that alone would give them integrity, turned to the question of cultural character, in effect turned back to the Chicago School, although he did not choose publicly to acknowledge this reversion. (However, in this and other papers, as well as in conversation, he was now prone to note that, after all these years, he was now speaking like his colleague at Chicago since 1945, Bernard Meland, who both in his own theology[34] and in his explicit accounts of the University of Chicago Divinity School[35] had done more than any other person to keep alive the spirit of the Chicago School.) Accordingly, Loomer's ''Notes'' reflect on recent American political, economic, and spiritual culture, and ask how one could make religious sense of that social reality. He asks repeatedly, what from a practical point of view can be done to respond to the failure of American culture? How can the Hebrew and Christian notions of community and love be utilized to change the social situation?

Loomer's pragmatic religious answer to the failure of the American ethos was an aesthetic answer, ''beauty as a design for life.'' Comparing recent years with earlier years, Loomer said, ''I came to the deeper conclusion that the basic category of value is stature or size, that stature is the most incontrovertible form of self-evidence.''[36] Loomer was now using that category explicitly for social institutions, contending that the aim of the social institutions should be to promote size in the individual participant in society. ''The basic institutions of society should be reconstituted so as to promote'' the aim at greater size.[37] He was willing to argue pragmatically that the size-producing capacities were more important than the justice-producing capacities of society, for justice pursued in our present statureless society will probably do more than give the once-downtrodden their opportunity to be truly dehumanized, insensitive, and materialistic, the way the elites of today are. It is legitimate, then, to concentrate on the aesthetic question of size, despite its seeming irresponsibility.

Size, Loomer makes clear, is not a category that springs full-blown into the mind of the theologian. Rather, size ''is a function of relationships.''[38] Size is a value category engendered not by the theoretical imagination, but by observed relationships. Size is a right-brained and aesthetic category in that it is really known, not through

---

[33]The best single account of the theory of the Chicago School is in William J. Hynes, *Shirley Jackson Case and the Chicago School* (Chico CA: Scholars Press, 1981).

[34]The best single example is Bernard E. Meland, *Fallible Forms and Symbols* (Philadelphia: Fortress Press, 1976).

[35]Principally, Bernard E. Meland, ''Introduction: The Empirical Tradition in Theology at Chicago,'' in *The Future of Empirical Theology,* ed. Bernard E. Meland (Chicago: The University of Chicago Press, 1969).

[36]Ibid., 15.

[37]Loomer, ''Notes,'' 16.

[38]Ibid.

moral or rational concepts, but through the intensity felt by an individual. That aesthetic intensity derives from the breadth and depth of relationships external to the self. This is to say that the idea of size is not a speculative category; it is an empirical generalization about the experience of relationships.

Loomer's change from a focus on the symbol of integrity to a focus on the symbol of size came about not only by a movement from rationalism to empiricism, but also by a shift away from the phenomenon of process to the phenomenon of relationality. Loomer's earlier theological efforts, even when they discussed empiricism, tended to focus on the structures of becoming, of process. In a lecture given at Saint John's University in 1979, "Process Theology: Origins, Strengths, Weaknesses," Loomer reports that he was named by Charles Hartshorne as the inventor of the label, "process theology." He goes on to say that if he is guilty of that, "it was an error and mistake of my youth, and I have been spending my latter days repenting."[39] The problem is that merely to substitute becoming for being as an ultimate metaphysical category would be like merely substituting Einstein for Newton; while Einstein and "becoming" are closer to the truth, they add refinements which are not always needed or, by themselves, fundamental to ordinary living. Rather, "It is relationships, and what they are about, that process is all about. Process is—as it were, exists—for the sake of the kinds of relationships that are creative of individuals and societies."[40] The truth of the processive character of reality is unimportant apart from the relational value that is generated within the process, and that value felt in relations Loomer came to describe with the term *size*. Accordingly, Loomer in his latter years recommended replacing the title "process theology" with "process-relational theology" and "process philosophy" with "process-relational philosophy."[41]

Loomer's concentration on relationality can be traced back at least to 1975 and his "Two Concepts of Power." His essay compares the two kinds of power that exist in relationships, unilateral power and relational power. Unilateral (or linear) power is the capacity to produce intended effects. It is one-sided and noncommunal, in that it involves what an active entity does to a passive entity. It is problematic because it is clearly nonmutual; my success with unilateral power means your failure, and vice versa. Loomer illustrates the concrete workings of unilateral power in sports, in relations between the rich and the poor, in relations between men and women, in politics, and in the dynamics of personal freedom. Loomer's notion of relational power is not simply the opposite of unilateral power; it is not simply the capacity to endure passively the effects of others. Loomer has no intention of substituting a stereotypical masculine power with a stereotypical feminine power. Rather, relational power is both

---

[39]Bernard M. Loomer, "Process Theology: Origins, Strengths, Weakness," a lecture given at Saint John's University, 1979, 1. See also Loomer, "The Future of Process Philosophy," in *Process Philosophy: Basic Writings,* ed. Jack R. Sibley and Pete A. Y. Gunter (Washington: University Press of America, 1978) 518: "In some place or other Charles Hartshorne generously credits me with possibly having baptized this mode of thought with the name 'process philosophy.' "

[40]Ibid., 2.

[41]For a second discussion of the switch, see Bernard M. Loomer, "The Future of Process Philosophy," in *Process Philosophy: Basic Writings,* 518.

active and passive: it is the active power required to sustain an identity while suffering widely divergent effects. It is ''the capacity to sustain a mutually internal relationship.''[42] *Size* is the term used to measure this power: ''Size is fundamentally determined by the range and intensity of internal relationships one can help create and sustain. The largest size is exemplified in those relationships whose range exhibits the greatest compatible contrasts, contrasts which border on chaos.''[43] ''The world of the individual who can be influenced by another without losing his or her identity or freedom is larger than the world of the individual who fears being influenced.''[44]

In effect, the essay, through an analysis of the experience of love, analyzes the empirical sources of size. Implicitly, Loomer questions the venerated concept of the purely active agape, the great Western concept of unilateral love. He replaces the paradigm of agape with the paradigm of size. The aesthetics of size should replace the moralism of agape, but Loomer never elaborated in detail on such an aesthetics.

In his last years Loomer talked frequently of writing a Christology. A combination of factors seems to have prevented that, but in his 1975 lecture, ''The Holocaust and Theology,'' there are hints of the direction he would have taken. Following Rosemary Radford Ruether, Loomer suggests that the centuries-old anti-Semitism follows from an equally old anti-Judaism that follows from something typically inherent in Christian theology: the claim that Jesus Christ is the absolute, final, unsurpassable revelation of God. Given this, Judaism is a mistake and an affront. This approach assumes, however, that ''our fondest hopes and cravings, those involving our conceptions of completion and final resolution and victory'' are to be honored.[45] Loomer suggests that this simple acceptance of our own agenda flies in the face of the evidence that not only our questions, but also our answers, are superseded in this emergent world. Jesus' power, Loomer argues, lies not in his final manifestation of an ideal, but in his capacity to enter into relation with those around him—not to shape the world to fit his own truth, but to influence and to be influenced by others. Among other things, this relational power means accepting the hatred of others without responding in kind; it means placing reconciliation above all else; and it means acquiring a strength that inevitably will call forth others' resentment, even violent resentment. Jesus' life demonstrates that ''relationships constitute the very stuff of our natural and historical existence, both as individuals and societies.''[46] Love is a value because it demonstrates this condition, and not the other way around; and Jesus is the Christ because he exercises this love, not because this love is the dictate of an unsurpassable meaning or a divine nature. Finally, because relations emerge in the process of life, every particular Christ and every particular revelation will always be surpassed. Jesus, however, is the Christ for a particular community because he ''was

---

[42]Bernard Loomer, ''Two Concepts of Power,'' *Process Studies* 6 (Spring 1976): 22.

[43]Ibid., 29-30.

[44]Ibid., 18.

[45]Bernard M. Loomer, ''The Holocaust and Theology,'' a lecture (1975), 23.

[46]Ibid., 17.

a disclosure and embodiment of size" and because he contributed to the size of others.[47] For some Westerners he paradigmatically took into himself an enormous diversity of relations without losing his identity and his influence in the process. He expressed the size-creating side of the natural world, manifesting one side of the life of God. To see Jesus, in a Tillichian sense, as the final expression of absolute being is a trivialization. A closer look at Jesus, Loomer argued, indicates that if we pursue relations we are permitted no closure, "that God's active presence amongst us permits of no definitive or final embodiment." "On the contrary. The mystery only deepens and evolves into more complex relations and dimensions."[48]

Whatever Loomer's particular changes in the 1970s, the larger shifts are from integrity to size, from a rationalistic emphasis to an empirical emphasis, from the criterion of coherence to the criterion of beauty, and from process to process-relationalism. The effects of those changes are nowhere more evident than in Loomer's "Size of God."

II   Implications

Loomer was not a particularly scholarly theologian. He did not seem to be the sort of person who was haunted by the possibility that he had not provided sufficient documentation, that some crucial writing was missing from his footnotes. Loomer's persuasion was more immediate and conversational; he seemed to rely on the cogency of his presentation. The texture of his writing grew more affective as he grew less rationalistic. For example, the use of stories became increasingly prominent in Loomer's writing.

That Loomer shunned the ordinary scholarly stance did not necessarily diminish his capacity as a significant observer and analyst of contemporary American culture. It could be argued that his concern for immediate persuasiveness was an attempt to gain greater access to the world he sought to describe, that neither the scholarly apparatus nor the theoretical constructs would be allowed to distance him from the observed world. Consistency with his own methodology—his radical, social, and historicist empiricism—could argue for such a direct and openly interpretive approach. If this were the case, then Loomer's conclusions stand in a significant relation with other recent trends of thought that aspire to report on the current cultural ethos. As it happens, in certain crucial particulars Loomer's thought does parallel that of recent deconstructionists, historicists, and neopragmatists.

It is all of a postmodernistic piece; it is all an effort to rely on experience rather than authority. If modernism is an effort begun in the sixteenth century to live without the authorization of the institutions of church, of Palestinian scriptures, of ancient Greeks, or of the monarchy, then postmodernism is the effort to live without the authorization that the moderns substituted for the premodern authorities. The rationalistic modernism initiated by Descartes issued in the idealism of Spinoza, Leibniz, Hegel, Husserl, and perhaps even Heidegger, all of whom authorized some structure of reason or held some

---

[47]Ibid., 13.

[48]Ibid., 16, 25.

ideal of pure thought. The empirical modernism traceable to Bacon, Hobbes, Locke, and Hume issued finally in the positivisms of Comte, Carnap, and Ayer, in the authorization of the scientific laws of the natural world. The subjectivist modernism initiated by Schleiermacher, Schopenhauer, and Kierkegaard issued in the egoisms of some of the phenomenologists and of existentialists, in the authorization of the self. Postmodernism is the effort to begin once more, to throw off the constraints of modernist authorization in order to permit what might be a more direct consideration of experience.

If it is viewed in terms of what it affirms, then postmodernism can be described in the language both of interpretation and of historicism. For postmodernism the act of interpretation literally constitutes both the past and the emerging present. Reality is composed of creaturely acts of interpreting the world; reality is the course of those interpretations that have composed the past and are now composing the present. Since the historical course of interpretation is the bottom reality, postmodernism can be called a historicism; but postmodernism is not simply a historicism, but a radical historicism in two senses. First, unlike the older historicisms of Dilthey, Hegel, Troeltsch, and Tillich, postmodernism does not treat history as the temporal window for some absolute or ultimate reality; instead, it treats the phenomena of history, the horizontal plane of history, as the last referent, beyond which there is no deeper reality. Second, unlike the historical positivisms typical of current cliometricians and of some social historians, the postmodernists are radical because they treat historical data the way William James treated empirical data when he exercised his method of "radical empiricism." The postmodernists have abandoned the preeminence of the five senses and the quantitative approach to reality. They have abandoned the fact-value dualisms that riddled empirical modernism; they are mind-body monists, as James was. History yields both facts and values, both the data of the positivist and the affectional realities of the humanist. The postmodernist historicism, then, is radical not only because it aims at nothing deeper than historical interpretations, but because these interpretations are thorough; they comprehend life rather than rearrange mere facts.

Loomer, like the deconstructionists, radical historicists, and neopragmatists, rejected modernist modes of scholarship and art.[49] Loomer also came to reject the rationalism in process philosophy, a rationalism that would attain clarity through the introduction of systematic thinking. For all the above-mentioned types of thinkers, including Loomer, we have only our own interpretation as a standpoint for making sense of the past, and the past itself is fundamentally a chain of interpretations—each generation interpreting an earlier generation, which interpreted an earlier generation. All of these thinkers in the last analysis share a kind of empiricist loyalty to history,

---

[49]By these rejections Loomer made a path parallel to that of Jacques Derrida, who has deconstructed the logocentrisms of Continental thought; and of neopragmatists such as Richard Rorty, Hilary Putnam, and Nelson Goodman, who have rejected their inherited American positivisms; and of Yale literary critics such as Hillis Miller, Paul de Man, and Geoffrey Hartman, who have rejected the ahistorical formalism of New Criticism; and of historicist literary critics such as Frank Lentricchia, who has rejected not only New Criticism, but even the cryptoformalism of the Yale Critics; and of physicists such as Neils Bohr and John Wheeler, who have rejected the rationalism of the relativity theory; and of poets such as William Carlos Williams and Charles Olson, who have rejected the traditionalisms of Eliot and Auden in favor of a fresh and interpretive appraisal of the "things" they confront in the world of ordinary experience.

even if history exists for them only as a chain of texts. There are no authorities transcending history.

For Loomer, as for his postmodernist collaborators, even the criterion for evaluating interpretations of history must be found in history. One must rely solely on the free interpretive act, loyal to the perceptions of the self, but loyal also to the outside limits the relational past seems to impose on interpretation. Yet these perceptions of the self and the limits of the past must be tested, for apart from this there is either a cryptotranscendentalization of the self or a cryptorationalization of history, and both are forms of authorization. Following James and Dewey, almost unconsciously, these postmodernists have the pragmatic test: to try a perception, to try a sense of limits, to try, in short, an interpretation in present society through conversation, through literary criticism, through the exchange of poetry, or through the use of relational power, but always to try within historical interaction.

Loomer's notion of size is finally a criterion of interpretation. It is a postmodern substitute for the rationalistic criterion of integrity. Loomer rejects modernism when he rejects the authority of rational integrity; he rejects the claim to evaluate thought and maturity by reference to "unities" in, with, and under the self or the world. Size is a category that rejects all extrahistorical referents, and it is a radically historicist criterion in three ways: first, it is realized in relation only with the diverse phenomena of the past; second, it assesses the past not primarily conceptually but primarily aesthetically—that is, with regard to qualities of experience; third, judgments of size are themselves tested pragmatically in history by asking whether what is claimed to have size truly combats the tedium of insufficient contrast on one hand, and on the other hand avoids excessive contrast (which destroys one's identity).

If it is accurate to say that Loomer's work is postmodern, this should not be in itself surprising. For his empirical, historicist position is traceable to his adoption of the attitude and often the explicit teachings of William James, John Dewey, and George Herbert Mead, let alone to the more empirical side of Whitehead. Richard Rorty, attempting to characterize the spirit of neopragmatism, has repeatedly cited James and Dewey as those who anticipated the entire development.[50] Further, Loomer's later theological work has been in the spirit of the Chicago School theologians, who themselves were heavily influenced by James, Dewey, and Mead.

III Evil

It is ironic that with the passing of years, particularly in the 1970s, Loomer's expatiations on the universality of ambiguity usually began with a nod to Reinhold Niebuhr. Loomer accepts as one of his own "basic principles" Niebuhr's notion that "every creative advance brings with it the possibility of greater evil."[51] Nevertheless, as Loomer recognized in his 1978 essay "The Future of Process Philosophy," Niebuhr himself would have rejected Loomer's own Christian naturalism because

---

[50]See, for example, Richard Rorty, *Consequences of Pragmatism* (Minneapolis: University of Minnesota Press, 1982) xviii.

[51]Loomer, "The Future of Process Philosophy," 536.

"God could not be identified with any natural or historical process because all such processes are ambiguous."[52]

The problem is compounded when one remembers that throughout the 1930s and 1940s Niebuhr attacked the naturalists. "The modern naturalist," Niebuhr announced, "whether romantic or rationalistic, has an easy conscience because he believes that he has not strayed very far from, and can easily return to, the innocency of nature."[53] Niebuhr also chastized the liberals of the Chicago School—Shailer Mathews and G. B. Smith in particular—for their "strikingly naive" understandings of history and for their "monotonous reiteration of the pious hope that people might be good and loving."[54] Yet finally it was Niebuhr who chose to contain evil, solidly walling it off from the Transcendent. Ironically, Niebuhr's own antinaturalism allowed him to limit the damage of evil in a way that many naturalists refused to limit it. Many old liberals of the Chicago School found evil in the only place they knew God, in the sociohistorical world; whereas Niebuhr diminished evil by denying that God is known only in the arena of an ambiguous history.

Loomer, with the intention of following to the end both the implication of naturalism and Niebuhr's doctrine of the sinful ambiguity of history, moved beyond his Christian naturalist colleagues in explicitly including God in the ambiguity of the world. If the naturalist's God must be found in the natural and historical process because that is the only world there is, and if Niebuhr is right about the sinful ambiguity of that process, then "naturalists have no choice but to opt for a God who is enmeshed in ambiguity." This is the price that is paid by one who aspires to what Loomer calls "the wisdom of the earth."

> This is the stance of one who is deeply attached to this life, this earth, this world. He believes that this is his home. Like the Jew, he trusts that the kingdom will come and that it will come here and not some place else. Or, rather, he may believe that it is always happening here, although its more complete exemplification lies in the future. He does not travel lightly. He brings all his traditions and relationships and hopes and meanings with him.[55]

Loomer contrasted the wisdom of the earth with the "wisdom of the pilgrim." "The pilgrim conceives himself as one for whom the earth is not his home. . . . He feels that the resources of earth and this life are not adequate for the living of it. The final resources must be derived from outside and beyond." The significant point here is the effects this latter wisdom has on the weight of evil: "When life comes to one of its many abysses, and meaning seems to have dissolved into nothingness, the pilgrim is not in complete despair because he has his way out, his escape hatch of transcen-

---

[52]Ibid.

[53]Reinhold Niebuhr, *The Nature and Destiny of Man: A Christian Interpretation* (New York: Charles Scribner's Sons, 1949) 1:104.

[54]Reinhold Niebuhr, *An Interpretation of Christian Ethics* (New York: Harper and Brothers Publishers, 1935) 173, 177.

[55]Loomer, "The Future of Process and Philosophy," 536.

dent meaning."[56] Although Loomer does not make the connection, it would seem that Niebuhr is himself a pilgrim. In the opening pages of Niebuhr's *The Nature and Destiny of Man* he says, "This essential homelessness of the human spirit is the ground of all religion; for the self which stands outside itself and the world cannot find the meaning of life in itself or the world."[57]

For Niebuhr, the self-styled realist, sin must be driven home as an awful, inevitable, and pervasive fact—but not so pervasive that it reaches everything, even God. For Loomer, who works in the company of reputedly optimistic naturalists, sin is thoroughly pervasive.

Loomer's concentration on the ambiguity between good and evil in natural, historical, and religious processes colors all his later thought. His notion of size, while it is an aesthetic category, goes beyond those formulas of aesthetics that identify the experience of beauty with a morally neutral unity amid diversity. For Loomer the aesthetics of size involves also the capacity to experience the diversity between good and evil. The person with greater size will be able to take within himself or herself greater evil and greater good without losing personal integrity. The person with size will be capable of knowing the highly private moral traumas of life in the twentieth-century West, the public tragedies of world wars, Third World poverty, and the threat of the loss of the human gene through nuclear war. He or she will oppose the forces that create these traumas and tragedies, and will recognize that they are inseparable from the forces that diminish those same traumas and tragedies; and this individual will act without losing identity. Accordingly, such an aesthetics of size should be directed toward those "educational, political, and economic institutions" that would work for the public good, for size-producing results in the public world.[58]

This sense of evil and the consequent sense of responsibility for one's own institutions seem to have lain beneath both periods (if the word is not too strong) of Loomer's professional life, beneath the paradigm of integrity as well as beneath the paradigm of size. Both senses were present in Loomer's more metaphysical concerns with Whitehead's cosmological scheme, when he applied the ideal of integrity to the problem of how the student and the divinity school could avoid the evils of mere competency. They were present in his earlier writings.[59] They were present in his efforts to attack the University of Chicago's collaboration with the military in its continuing involvement in nuclear research.[60] And they were present in his participation in a national campaign to prevent the execution of the Rosenbergs.[61] They may have been present even in his tendency to extend a three o'clock appointment with a student until 8:00 or 9:00 in the evening.

---

[56]Ibid., 536-537.

[57]Niebuhr, *Nature and Destiny,* 14.

[58]Loomer, "The Future of Process Philosophy," 538.

[59]See, for example, Bernard M. Loomer, "Ely on Whitehead's God," in *Process Philosophy and Christian Thought,* 283ff.; Loomer, "Christian Faith and Process Philosophy," ibid., 94-97.

[60]Bernard M. Loomer, "An Atomic Energy Proposal," *The University of Chicago Magazine* 73 (1979).

[61]See R. Scott Appleby, "The Divinity School Deans 1892-1960," *Criterion* 19 (Autumn 1980): 22.

Finally, though, Loomer was not shocked by evil because he held no vision of perfection. When that vision is relinquished, evil may remain real but appear less surprising. The result may be closer to religious modesty than to anything else. It may foster a suspicion of the intercontinental abstraction and a concern for the local.[62] Loomer's religious modesty may be best described by the American poet William Carlos Williams, who spent his life in Rutherford, New Jersey.[63] The last thing one would expect from two such energetic American characters is religious modesty. Nevertheless, Williams opens his epic *Paterson* with these lines:

> *To make a start,*
> *out of particulars*
> *and make them general, rolling*
> *up the sum, by defective means—*
> *Sniffing the trees,*
> *just another dog*
> *among a lot of dogs. What*
> *else is there? And to do?*
> *The rest have run out—*
> *after the rabbits.*
> *Only the lame stands—on*
> *three legs. Scratch front and back.*
> *Deceive and eat. Dig*
> *a musty bone*[64]

Bernard Loomer was to spend the rest of his life on the nation's other shore where his last public address was to be to the Pacific Coast Theological Society in October 1980. It ended with this sentence: "The question of the meaningfulness of life does not depend on whether nature in its behavior conforms even to the deepest hopes, needs, and aspirations of man."[65]

---

[62]Is it purely accidental that Loomer, a university intellectual, never left the United States except once, and then for less than a day in Mexico?

[63]Loomer and Williams, incidentally, use the same historically thick and radically empirical image in their sole prose writings on America: Williams's *In the American Grain* (New York: New Directions Books, 1956) and Loomer's "Theology in the American Grain," *The Universalist Christian* 30 (1975-1976): 23-34. Reprinted in *Process Philosophy and Social Thought,* ed. John B. Cobb, Jr. and W. Widick Schroeder (Chicago: Center for the Scientific Study of Religion, 1981) 141-52.

[64]William Carlos Williams, *Paterson* (New York: New Directions, 1963) 3.

[65]Bernard M. Loomer, "The Doctrine of Creation Revisited: A Theology of Nature," a lecture to the Pacific Coast Theological Society (1980) 5.

PUBLISHED WORKS BY BERNARD M. LOOMER

"Whitehead's Method of Empirical Analysis." *Process Theology: Basic Writings,* ed. E. H. Cousins, 67-82. New York: Newman Press,1971. [A selection from "The Theological Significance of the Method of Empirical Analysis in the Philosophy of A. N. Whitehead," 369-87. Ph.D. Dissertation, University of Chicago, 1942].

"Ely on Whitehead's God." *Journal of Religion* 24 (1944): 162-79. Repr. in *Process Philosophy and Christian Thought,* ed. D. Brown, R. E. James, Jr., and G. Reeves, 264-86. Indianapolis: Bobbs-Merrill, 1971.

"The Federated Theological Faculty." *The Divinity School News* 13 (1946): 1-3 [*The Divinity School News* of the University of Chicago Divinity School].

"Neo-Naturalism and Neo-Orthodoxy." *Journal of Religion* 28 (1948): 79-91. Portions reprinted in "New Framework for an Enduring Faith," *The Divinity School News* 15 (1948): 1-7.

"The Federated Theological Faculty Today." *The Chicago Theological Seminary Register* 39 (1949): 6-12.

"The Aim of Divinity Education." *The Divinity School News* 16 (1949): 1-6.

"Christian Faith and Process Philosophy." *Journal of Religion* 29 (1949): 181-203. Repr. in *Process Philosophy and Christian Thought,* 70-98.

"Religion and the Mind of the University." In *Liberal Learning and Religion,* ed. Amos N. Wilder, 147-68. New York: Harper, 1951.

"A Theology of Freedom." *Motive* (1953): 8-12.

"Man and His Universe: And the Nature of the Universe to Which He is Related." In *Religion in Higher Education,* 63-71. Mount Vernon IA: The Cornell College Press, 1954.

"Tillich's Theology of Correlation." *Journal of Religion* 36 (1956): 150-56.

"Reinhold Niebuhr's *The Self and the Dramas of History.*" *Pastoral Psychology* 9 (1958): 17-20.

"Reflections on Theological Education." *Criterion* 4 (1965): 3-8.

"Empirical Theology within Process Thought." In *The Future of Empirical Theology,* ed. Bernard E. Meland, 149-73. Chicago: University of Chicago Press, 1969.

"S-I-Z-E." *Criterion* 13 (1974): 5-8. Repr. in *Religious Experience and Process Theology,* ed. Harry James Cargas and Bernard Lee, 69-76. New York: Paulist Press, 1976.

"Remarks by Bernard M. Loomer." *Alumni* (published by The Divinity School of the University of Chicago) (1974): 1-4.

"Response to David R. Griffin." *Encounter* 36 (1975): 361-69.

"Theology in the American Grain." *The Unitarian-Universalist Christian* 30 (1975-1976): 23-34. Repr. in *Process Philosophy and Social Thought,* ed. John B. Cobb, Jr. and W. Widick Schroeder, 141-52. Chicago: Center for the Scientific Study of Religion, 1981.

"Dimensions of Freedom." In *Religious Experience and Process Theology,* 323-39.

"The Price of Greatness ('Ford to Nixon')." In *Religious Experience and Process Theology,* 341-45.

"Two Conceptions of Power." *Process Studies* 6 (1976): 5-32.

"The Free and Relational Self." In *Belief and Ethics,* ed. W. Widick Schroeder, 69-86. Chicago: Center for the Scientific Study of Religion, 1978.

"The Future of Process Philosophy." In *Process Philosophy: Basic Writings,* ed. Jack R. Sibley and Pete A. Gunter, 513-38. Washington: University Press of America, 1978.

"The Web of Life." In *The Nature of Life,* ed. William Heidcamp, 93-109. Baltimore: University Park Press, 1978.

"An Atomic Energy Proposal." *The University of Chicago Magazine* 73 (1979): 21-26.

"Dores R. Sharpe: Portrait of a Christian Rebel." *Foundations: A Baptist Journal of History and Theology* 24 (1981): 99-121.

"Meland on God." *American Journal of Theology & Philosophy* 5 (1984): 138-43.

"A Process-Relational Conception of Creation." In *Cry of the Environment: Rebuilding the Christian Creation Tradition,* ed. Philip Jornason and Ken Butigan, 321-28. Sante Fe NM: Bear & Co., 1984.

Unfoldings: Conversations from the Sunday Morning Seminars of Bernie Loomer. Berkeley CA: First Unitarian Church, 1985.

THE SIZE OF GOD

Bernard M. Loomer

Abstract

This is an essay on certain aspects of God's stature. The philosophic mode of thought is process-relational and the method is rational-empirical. The emphasis is naturalistic. The essay proceeds in terms of the general contention that if the one world, the experienceable world with its possibilities, is all the reality accessible to us, then one conclusion seems inevitable: God is to be identified either with a part or with the totality of the concrete, actual world. The thesis of my essay is that God should be identified with the totality of the word, with whatever unity the totality possesses.

The fundamental propositions of the essay are the following:

1. The self-sufficiency of the world enshrouds the inexhaustible mystery inherent with the actual world.

2. Order is an abstraction from the interconnectedness of events.

3. Love is grounded upon interconnectedness, rather than the other way around.

4. The widest generalization of the principle of interconnectedness results in the conception of the world as a web of interconnected events.

5. The unity of the world is the unity of this societal web of interrelatedness.

6. The perfection of a God derived from a priori considerations is the perfection of high abstractions. As concretely actual, God (or the world) is ambiguous.

7. The unity of the world conceived as a universal order (or God defined as a principle of order) leads to a theology or philosophy of abstractionism.

8. Christian doctrines of God and Christology have been shaped by their passion for perfection or the unambiguous, but the unambiguous has the status of an abstraction. The concretely real is ambiguous. An ambiguous God is of greater stature than an unambiguous deity.

9. Process-relational thought has been notable in its efforts to overcome the various bifurcations of modern philosophy, but the major exponents of this mode of thought exemplify the ultimate bifurcation—that between good and evil.

10. Whitehead does this by ontologically separating God and creativity.

11. Wieman does this by defining God as one process among others, a God of creative transformation. Both views result in making God an abstraction.

12. The basic theological and philosophical tradition of the West has maintained that the answer to the ambiguities of life is some form of unambiguity. In terms of this essay this translates into the notion that the answer to life is death.

13. The creative advance of the world is not to be understood as an adventure toward perfection. Rather, this advance is a struggle toward greater stature.

14. Ambiguity should perhaps be understood as a metaphysical principle.

The context of the present topic consists in the transition from a theology that maintains that resources for salvation ultimately derive from a transcendent God to an outlook that suggests that the graces for the living of a creative life emerge within the depths and immediacies of concrete experience. It is a transition from the wisdom of the sojourner, who was made in the image of his[1] creator and who travels lightly through his terrestrial pilgrimage because his destiny is a transcendent home, to the wisdom of the evolved earth-creature, whose spirit had its origin in the flames of the stars and the dust of the planet, whose home is the earth, whose destiny, or that of his descendents, may be extinction or life among the stars, and whose fulfillment as an individual and as a species requires a deep attachment to the humanizing processes of this life.

These transitions are aspects of a more basic shift in perspective from the two worlds of traditional thought to the one evolved and relativized world of contemporary imagery. This movement entails a revolution in our conception of the life of God and of our participation in it.

The God of our fathers was an infinite God; His qualities were defined in terms of the uttermost forms of perfection. Sometimes these superlatives were character-

---

[1]This essay was published with Bernard Loomer's approval and cooperation, but its final editing occurred after his death. While it is the policy of Mercer University Press and of the *American Journal of Theology & Philosophy* to ask their authors to substitute gender-inclusive language for gender-specific language, this was impossible here. Under the circumstances the editors did not feel entitled on their own to introduce gender-inclusive language and the required concomitant word changes in the many instances where that would have been appropriate.

ized by means of the negation of the limits of human attributes. He transcended us in all respects. Whatever limitations He possessed or operated with were self-imposed. He was the primordial source of all good, and the incommensurate standard by which all our thoughts, actions, and virtues were to be judged and found wanting. He knew about evil, and He sometimes made use of it in the process of achieving His purpose. But His character and actions, while many-faceted, were wholly unambiguous.

This God was personal, loving, merciful, and gracious. He was also free and creative. He made a world that was wholly dependent on His power and sufferance for its continued existence, but he was not identified with this world. He transcended the world in somewhat the same manner in which an artist transcends his creation. The object (as an artistic creation) is derived from the artist's creativity, and something of the spirit of the artist is exemplified in his creation; but the being of the artist is quite independent of the existence of the work of art that he created.[2] So God transcended the world, although both His creative activity and His redemptive work in and through Jesus Christ somehow manifested His infinite wisdom, His incomparable goodness, and His adequate power. (The ways in which all this and more have been revealed and vouchsafed in the person, work, and life of Jesus have never been adequately explained in the annals of Christian theology.)

For the purposes of this discussion, it must be emphasized that God in His being was totally independent of the being of the world and its creatures. This basic distinction between God and the world has been fundamental throughout the history of Christian theology. I suggest that this is a pivotal point in looking at the traditional picture of God. His status as God, and His worthiness of our worship and commitment, were not grounded on religious and ethical factors alone, abstracted from all metaphysical considerations. God was not only the author of our salvation, the forgiver of our sins, and the one who established the new as well as the old covenant; He was also the lord of history and the maker of heaven and earth. The concept of lordship includes the notion that the fundamental conditions of our natural and historical existence—such as sexuality, mortality, and the feeding of species on other species—were derived from the wisdom and power of God. Without these qualities of lordship and transcendent creativity, God would not have had the status of being the one universal God by whose power all things were made and continue to exist. God was love, and love was of God as a fundamental quality of His being, but love was not the being of God. The being of God was the being of independent, transcendent self-existence; the being of God was His aseity.

I hazard the judgment that God's freedom, His unambiguous goodness, and even His holiness derived in large part from the independence of His being.

With the elimination of the transcendental world of metaphysical independence, first causes, perfection, aseity, and preestablished unity, a radical shift occurs. If the one world, the experienceable world with its possibilities, is all the reality accessible

---

[2]The artist, as artist, may not be completely independent of his artistic creativity, although he transcends any one expression of it; but the artist as a whole person transcends both his artistic creativity and the results of his work.

to us, as naturalists claim, then one conclusion seems inevitable. If God is to be spoken of as something more than an ideal or a principle (that is, as something more than a final or formal cause), then it follows that the being of God must be identified in some sense with the being of the world and its creatures. To express the point in naturalistic categories: If God has a reality beyond that of an abstraction, then God is in some sense concretely actual. As an actuality or a group of actualities God is then to be identified either with a part or with the totality of the concrete, actual world, including its possibilities.

The following discussion is devoted to a partial exploration of one option within this general thesis: the alternative that God is to be identified with the totality of the world. More particularly, the focus is on the character and stature of God in relation to His concrete actuality. It represents another effort to characterize the reality and limits of a finite and concrete God. The inquiry moves within the orbit of a type of thought that began with the work of Henri Bergson and William James and includes the thought of A. N. Whitehead as its major metaphysical embodiment. I describe it as a process-relational mode of thinking. The present discussion continues the empirical tradition within this general understanding of the nature of things. It was James who suggested in 1907 that "some kind of an immanent or pantheistic working *in* things rather than above them is, if any, the kind recommended to our contemporary imagination."[3]

I take note that there are many who will contend that naturalism, especially the type I will attempt to outline briefly, is incompatible with Christian faith. If the Christian faith is understood as a tradition that permits no radical transformation of itself, I would agree with the contention. This is not the occasion to suggest a possible justification in Christian terms of the general orientation with which I stand. Suffice it to say that I am attempting to do theologically what Whitehead suggested should be done philosophically, namely, to take a set of ideas, the best that one has, and unflinchingly to explore experience with the aid of those ideas. To do so "unflinchingly" suggests the quality of courage that is required in this venture, especially when the inquiry takes place in unfamiliar and traditionally forbidden territory, and when the tentative conclusions may appear to be so at odds with what has been accepted as true and adequate and helpful for so long. (Tillich, for example, has called the position that I find myself driven to "absurd.") I assume that courage and tentativity, along with humility, are inherent qualities of faith. At least this inquiry is undertaken in this spirit.

The Naturalistic Outlook

The naturalistic outlook that is operative within this inquiry can be expressed in terms of basic empirical, methodological principles, or at least those that are most pertinent to the discussion. These principles do not have an independent justification; they are of a piece with the accompanying ontological stance. They are in fact the methodological expression of this ontology, since the ontology is embodied in their

---

[3]William James, *Pragmatism* (London, New York, Toronto: Longmans, Green and Co., 1940) 70.

content. The spirit of these principles exemplifies the methodological and ontological humility characteristic of much of modern thought since the time of Hume and Kant.

1. There is the general empirical principle that knowledge is derived from and confirmed by physical experience. This entails the notion that ideas are primarily reflective of physical or bodily experience, although they may also be elicited secondarily from other ideas that in turn are ultimately rooted in physical experience.

Physical experience is a generative and formative encounter with concrete actualities existing in the context of the immediate past of an emerging subject (including the subject's past self). This experience involves a causal feeling of derivation from influences issuing from the past. As data, these influences do not include past actualities in their concrete fullness. The formed energies of past actualities are objectified in the mode of perspectives of themselves.[4] These perspectives are projected as vectors into the present and become the causal data from which present actualities are created. Physical experience is at once an act of perception and a process of creation whereby the present actuality emerges as a synthesis of its constitutive past world.

Physical feelings are the fundamental avenues through which we meet and absorb the elemental forces of our existence. They are the primary mode in which we experience the processive and relational as well as the qualitative (especially the affectional and evaluative) dimensions of life. The heights and depths of life, the unmanageable and efficacious undertows of existence, and the transformative energies of creative interchange are known first through our bodily feelings.

Sense perception, by contrast, is an abstract version of physical experience. It is a perception of contemporaneous sensorial forms and qualities, together with their mathematical relations, in abstraction from the presupposed causal matrix of concrete actualities of which they are ostensible components. It is a more specialized type of prehension that enables us to have relatively clear and distinct impressions of the more manageable features of our experience.

Conceptual experience is a complex phenomenon. On the one hand, it is an envisagement of structures, forms, and qualities (including novel instances of these entities) in their capacity for being determinative elements in the creation of concrete actualities. The scope of this envisagement may range from relevant solutions to immediate practical problems, and even to the farthest reaches of imagination and speculative thought. A conceptual sensitivity to relationships and interconnectedness is the basis for theoretical generalization.

On the other hand, all physical experience involves some degree of conceptual response. These responses are interpretations and evaluations of physical experience. They heighten or diminish the intensity of physical feelings. They enhance or distort the reality of these primal forces. In these and other ways conceptual operations advance or weaken the organismic freedom of actual realities.

---

[4]We are accustomed to think that a standpoint determines a perspective, but in this interpretation of physical experience perspectives objectified from the past determine a standpoint in the present. The past perspectivizes itself. These perspectives are abstractions from the past, but they are physical rather than conceptual in nature.

An intuition in the perceptual sense is a physical experience with a modicum of conceptual interplay. The far-ranging insights of religious intuitions are derived from the fusion of physical and conceptual sensitivity to life-directive and life-transformative qualities and relationships.

2. The extensiveness and dimensions of our knowledge are determined by the range and depth of our experience. The limits of the knowable are defined in terms of what is experienceable (including the possibility of parapsychological phenomena). The limits of what is experienceable are constituted by the boundaries of our relationships with other realities, both actual and possible. These relationships are the media through which other realities affect or communicate with us.

3. The disavowal of transcendental causes, principles, and explanations is the negative side of the assertion of the self-sufficiency of the world and of our descriptive analysis of it. Whitehead's version of this point states that "there is an essence to the universe which forbids relationships beyond itself, as a violation of its reality."[5] This statement is sometimes, I think, mistakenly interpreted in rationalistic terms.

4. This naturalistic orientation can be restated in terms of a principle that is both methodological and ontological in scope: the reasons why things are the way they are and behave as they do are to be found within the things themselves and their relationships (including the factor of chance) to each other.[6] The "reasons" are conceptual abstractions from the functionings of concrete actualities. In this sense ultimate explanations are descriptions expressed in their most generalized form. In Whitehead's words, "explanation is the analysis of coordination."[7]

5. Actual entities are not created by combining formal abstractions. A concrete individual is never "possible." "Philosophy is explanatory of abstractions and not of concreteness. . . . Creativity is the ultimate behind all forms, inexplicable by forms" (Whitehead).[8]

6. The self-sufficiency of the world of our experience enshrouds the unfathomable or inexhaustible mystery inherent within the factuality of the world.

The irreducibility of the fundamental premises of our description of the nature of things defines the limits of human inquiry. The reasonableness of these hard-won premises (whether from revelation or reason or empirical analysis) is an apparent assurance of the measure of our grasp of ultimate meaning. We may be impelled to believe that our deepest and dearest convictions concerning value and the "way of things" penetrate to the very heart and mind of the "why of things," or that the innermost secret of the world is decisively disclosed in the very structure of the world that we have described in our categories, or that our necessary and primordial truths reverberate with confirmation throughout the abyss of meaning.

---

[5]Alfred North Whitehead, *Process and Reality: An Essay in Cosmology,* ed. David Ray Griffin and Donald Sherburne (New York: Free Press, 1978) 4.

[6]Whitehead's "ontological principle," which states that to look for reasons is to look for actual entities, is another rendering of the general empirical principle.

[7]Ibid., 153.

[8]Ibid., 20.

It may be so; and we must live with the aid of the wisdom we have. But awe and wonder, which constitute the rich soil in which wisdom flourishes, are not exhausted by revelations, necessary truths, and self-evident premises upon which intellectual worlds are erected. They are the primal exemplifications of self-transcendence.

The unremovable, intellectual arbitrariness of the premises of meaning that undergird our systems of explanation symbolizes the immanence of the mystery of existence that absorbs not only our questions but also our deep-rooted criteria of value and intelligibility. This absorption is reflected back to us both as an affirmation and as a beckoning beyond ourselves. Our deepest wisdom is productive of a peace consonant with our understanding. It is also generative of a restiveness that impels us toward a fullness or an emergent "more" that lies beyond our comprehension.

Faith seeks an understanding of itself, and trust requires some sense of vindication. Yet the depth of trust that tries to assimilate the tortuous turnings and baffling agonies of experience outruns the assurance of either self-evident understanding or the vindication of prior fulfillment.

The basic ontological categories are relatively few in number. There is, in the first place, the fact of becoming; but becomingness is not a substantive entity in itself. Like all categories, it exists only in terms of its exemplifications. There are only specific instances of becoming, or particular units of process; there is no creativity apart from the creativity of individual units of actuality. Furthermore, there are no instances of bare or contentless becoming. Process is the becoming of experience, and these instances of becoming are occasions of experience. They are somewhat analogous to James's "drops" of experience.

These occasions of experience are the fundamental actualities of the world, the concrete individuals that constitute the successive moments in the historic lives of all forms and levels of existence. These occasions are the subjects of their experience. Their subjective experience is a synthetic process of unifying the several forms of vectorial energy derived from past occasions.[9] Their subjective individuality, their self-creativity, and their freedom consist in the manner of their response to what they have received. This is their "howness" of becoming, or the style and spirit of their life: How they become determines what they become.

Viewed from another standpoint, these occasions of experience are what and where they become. Their subjective experience occurs when and where it does, and once having become something definite within a particular spatial and temporal context they do not move or change. They cannot move or change. They can only be

---

[9]Whitehead holds that his irreducible quanta of energy are the "final" subjects, the elemental individuals, and that all other, more complex organizations of energy are either nexuses or societies. Whitehead may be metaphysically correct, even though the empirical truth-status of his position may be moot, or must await future means of verification. But this issue aside, the precise application of his distinction and concepts to all situations and kinds of problems makes discussion needlessly awkward and cumbersome. In terms of this essay, we can make the kinds of distinctions within the world of reality that are most relevant to the kind of problem and type of inquiry under consideration. For our purposes these occasions or drops of experience vary in their extensiveness. The fundamental definition of an individual unit of concrete actuality is that it is a process of unification, whether or not it includes other and smaller processes of becoming.

superseded. They inherit only from the past and, having etched their individual stamp on their inheritance, for richer or poorer, they project their decision into the future.

The instances of the becoming of individuals are transient and episodic in their duration. They are superseded by other instances so as to form a historic and causal route of occasions. (Change occurs only within this route.) This route of successive individuals or occasions of experience will be termed an event. The concept of events is useful because it enables us to deal with organizations of energy of greater complexity and extensiveness than actual occasions of experience exemplify. In everyday usage, when we refer to an individual, we normally have in mind an enduring person, and not a self as a momentary occasion. Most of the basic affairs of our common life are carried on in terms of relatively permanent and complex personages. The decisive sections of this essay will be concerned with individuals in their more extended reality—that is, as events. An event is an ''enduring individual.''

An individual instance of becoming is shaped (in large part) by past occasions upon which it is dependent and from which it emerges. Because of this dependence its relation to its past is internal. But it is independent of its contemporaries. It neither influences nor is directly influenced by them. Because of this independence it is externally related to its present. Because of its perspectival projections of itself it can help to shape the future. However, it is independent of the future, since as a past occasion it cannot be altered. Thus its relation to future occasions is also external. With respect to individual occasions of experience the line of dependence is asymmetrical or unilateral. As transient moments of subjectivity they do not participate in relationships of interdependence. This lack of mutual dependence provides a context within which they can exercise whatever degree of freedom they possess.

The relationship of interdependence obtains only between several routes of occasions, or events, that perdure over an indefinite, yet sizeable, temporal span. These routes are, for the most part, roughly contemporaneous with each other. In this essay where I speak of interdependence and interconnectedness, the reference will be to individuals or persons as events, and not to individuals as momentary occasions.[10] In this fashion the freedom of individuals as occasions, and the externality of many of their relationships, are maintained within the context of the interdependence of events.

Finally, concrete occasions and events should be distinguished from material objects that we see, such as bridges, trees, and people. Occasions are particular processes of the becoming of individuals as subjects, as selves. Events are durational, historic routes of successive occasions. Material objects are the enduring or recurring structures within events. The distinction between an event and a material object corresponds to the difference between an extended process (or an extended succession

---

[10]The use of ''individual'' to indicate both a momentary self and an enduring person may be confusing, but the text and the context should make it clear which connotation is intended. This possible confusion could be avoided by always using the term *event* when speaking of interdependence and reserving the term *individual* when speaking of the momentary self. In addition to the consideration that this does not conform to ordinary usage, there are significant dimensions of meaning carried by the phrase ''interdependent individuals'' that cannot be conveyed by the expression ''interconnected events,'' although this latter phrase will also be employed at times, especially when a more general reference is intended.

of processes) and an enduring structure. The fundamental concrete reality is the process or the occurrence and the structure is an abstract component of the occurrence.

In the language of this essay, a person may be defined as an enduring object (actually, an incredibly complex society of countless enduring objects) when we have reference primarily to his formal or structural characteristics which are maintained over a considerable stretch of time. A person may also be defined as an extended event (again, of baffling complexity) when we intend to suggest the dynamic basis of his sustained existence.

All organizations of energy into groups that exemplify some causal connections are, strictly speaking, organizations of events and not simply of transient occasions. Contemporaneous occasions are mutually independent. Causal connections involve the temporal relationship of "earlier" and "later." This means that any structural grouping must include several sequences (events or enduring objects) wherein the earlier phase in any one sequence influences the later phases in other sequences.[11]

So, secondly, events create (and are created by) two kinds of enduring groups, a nexus and a society. A nexus is a relatively unorganized relational matrix of interconnected events whose members manifest a spatial togetherness. A society is a nexus whose members illustrate a common mode or behavior or feeling. This commonality of behavior (which may be quite simple or complex in its structure) is the "defining characteristic" of the group. This distinguishing feature is inherited by each member through its causal or determining relations with other members of the web.

Whether we move toward the larger or the smaller, obviously there are societies within societies. The more inclusive the society the more abstract and vague its defining characteristic. Communities constitute a species of society with a more deeply etched commonality of spirit.

Thirdly, occasions of experience and events exemplify the physical, sensual, emotional, and purposive dimensions of life. These are the various qualities with which we encounter the energy in its unadorned factuality. As Henry Nelson Wieman put it: Energy always comes to us clothed in qualities such as softness, yellow, or joy.

Fourthly, occasions are largely constituted by their relationships with other occasions. Relationships are the realities through which we encounter each other and become members one of another. They constitute the situational contexts or fields in which we live, move, and have our being.

Finally, the fact of order indicates the structures of organization that are exemplified within occasions and events, and the patterns of relationship between events.

We have, then, a perspective on the nature of things that emphasizes the ultimacy of becoming and the primacy of relationships. I will return to this topic shortly, but

---

[11]Whitehead's discussion of the concepts of nexus and society is puzzling. He is heavily insistent on the causal independence of contemporaries. Yet he characterizes both of these groups in terms of prehensions among their members, which are actual entities or occasions. But physical prehensions occur in physical time for Whitehead. They are in fact the very temporality of physical time. Thus there can be no nexuses or societies simply of occasions. These two groups presuppose successions of occasions, if they are to exemplify prehensive connections. Nexuses and societies are temporal or enduring groupings. In this sense an "enduring society" is redundant.

I conclude this preliminary discussion by underlining certain basic features of this point of view.

Because of our long substantialist tradition in philosophy and theology it is difficult to avoid thinking that there is another substratum of reality that undergirds the world of events. This notion seems to add a dimension of meaning and a depth of value that a purely naturalistic outlook appears to lack. Possibly so. Yet, in terms of this essay, there is nothing beyond processive actualities. The occasion itself (and its constitutive relations) is the fundamental reality. Events do not occur to something that is not itself an event, an occasion of experience is not an incident in the life of a self who is not an occasion. The self is its occasion, and the enduring person is a historic route of such occasions.

In this view there is no ground of being that is the source of all becoming but, in itself, is not becoming. The only ground for the becoming of an actuality consists of other, temporally prior actualities from which the energy of its becoming is derived.

Similarly, the referents of such terms as power, freedom, and creativity should not be reified. There is no independent or self-existing power beyond that of individuals and societies existing in a relational matrix. Freedom is not a preformed, spiritual reality from which we can draw our resources. Creativity is not an entity, either actual or possible. These concepts refer to qualities of concrete particulars. Grammatically these terms are nouns, but, with the possible exception of creativity, they function as adverbs. They are not "whats" but "hows." They are indicative of modes of behaviors of actual occasions.

Even these concrete actualities, while they have the grammatical status of nouns, should be classified more accurately as verbs. When we refer to them as nouns, I suggest that we have reference to the relative permanence of an enduring historic route of occasions, or to some structure of formed identity that we derive by abstraction from the ebb and flow of transient occasions of experience.

The point of these concluding introductory remarks concerns the viability of this outlook as a living option. Within the fundamental pluralism of this position there is the inherent claim that the heights and depths of existence, including the qualities of profound religious encounters and the resources for living an abundantly meaningful life, are to be experienced within the concrete realities of this world. This contention conjoins the sense of ultimacy in meaning and the immediacy of experienceable actualities (to borrow Bernard Meland's language).

The translation of this mode of thought into a style of life is premised upon what may be called an "attachment to life." I have described this stance elsewhere[12] as a persistent and spirit-testing commitment to the specific processes of life, as a "discerning immersion in what is most deeply present at hand and concretely at work in our midst."[13] The cultivation of this commitment is the elemental reason for an empirical emphasis in theology and philosophy.

---

[12]Bernard Loomer, "The Future of Process Philosophy," in *Process Philosophy: Basic Writings,* ed. Jack R. Sibley and Pete A. Y. Gunter (Washington: University Press of America, 1978) 537-38.

[13]Ibid., 537. This immersion is to be informed by various forms of understanding, including Marxist, existential, and psychoanalytic perspectives.

The importance of empirical method depends on the value that is assigned to our existential assimilation of those life-determining processes and relations that are (or ought to be) the focus of empirical inquiry in theology and philosophy. Charles Hartshorne contends that metaphysical truth is a priori truth, and that the practice of empirical method in metaphysics results in our being unable to make any significant distinctions between metaphysics and science. With some important qualifications, this contention may be granted. But truth exists for the sake of value. The value that is at stake in a commitment of attachment is the value of the relational life in its deepest meaning. This meaning (for us) is symbolized by the cross. The discipline of this way of life involves the most mature sensitivity to the workings of concrete processes in the context of internal relations. (This discipline is surely one of the greatest challenges for the human spirit.) This essay contends that an empirical stance is more helpful in promoting and deepening an attachment to the concrete processes of life. All articulated truth is abstract. Therefore, a priori truth is doubly abstract. The grandeur of abstractions is their capacity to extend the intellectual horizons of our lives; but this grandeur is ambiguous, for the pursuit of these abstractions also lures us away from the sensitive immersion in concrete processes that an attachment to life requires.

An attachment to life does not preclude a gladsome and ample appreciation of the wide-ranging functions of reason. The exemplification of a generality of thought is an indispensable feature of any high civilization. It is an agent in the purifying and humanizing of our physical feelings. Most important, an openness to conceptual novelty is a vital element in one kind and level of transformation.

But for all its impressive importance conceptual openness is an abstract way of being accessible to change. This is a receptivity to form. A deeper type of openness is a receptivity to the concrete processes involving causal relationships, especially those that are mutually internal. This kind of openness issues in a more organic type of transformation.

There are alternative modern conceptions of the nature and source of the directive that should guide modern man's efforts to help shape the course of human history. For some this directive is indigenous to the dynamic and controlling thrust of scientific knowledge and technological advances. For others it is derived from an existential self-consciousness as it confronts the structure of alienation and the threats of nothingness inherent within our various societies. For still others it is to be found within the insights and ideals of our rational understanding (in both its idealistic and humanistic modes) in its efforts at creative ecological reconstruction, and for some others it is exemplified in the various methods for heightening the psychic and spiritual level of human consciousness as preparation for the next stage in the evolution of the human spirit.

From the standpoint of this essay neither self-consciousness nor knowledge can provide an adequate directive for the reformation of society or the evolution of the human spirit. They can provide conditions that can facilitate or frustrate the working of the directive, but the directive is to be found within those processes involved in sustained, mutually internal relations. The "wisdom" that can be trusted, and the kind of power consistent with this wisdom, are contained within, or emerge from, these relationships.

Given the outline of the resources available to our inquiry, the thesis will be developed in terms of four topics: the web of life, the unity of the web, the concept of ambiguity, and the creative advance.

The Web of Life

The basic perspective that I have outlined in the introduction has been identified as "process philosophy," and theologians working within this mode of thought have identified themselves as "process theologians." Apart from the point that the religious base of these theologians does not derive in the first instance from this philosophic stance (although I do contend that it has made fundamental contributions to our religious understanding), I want to stress the importance of relationships. If the role of relationships is underplayed in this perspective, an ontology of becoming will have been substituted for an ontology of being, which could be compared to the difference between Einstein and Newton. The cutting edge of this mode of thought results from the synthesis of becoming and relationality.

If we speak of the ultimacy of becoming, then we must speak of the primacy of relatedness. Becoming may be the more inclusive category, but without the presence of dynamic relationships from which actualities emerge, the notion of becoming would be empty of content. Neither becoming nor relatedness is an emergent. They are equiprimordial.[14]

Furthermore, even though becoming is the most inclusive category, relatedness has a priority in value. Process exists for the sake of relationships. The final justification for taking the notion of process as the basic category is teleological. It is a way of stating and grounding the conviction that at the heart of things there is a passion or a restlessness to move toward the increase in value, to achieve the "more," to transform what is into a "better." This means there is a drive to create those kinds of relationships from which more complex individuals and societies of greater stature may emerge.

In this perspective, actualities are largely constituted by their relations. Relations are the carriers of energy projected from past occasions, from which present occasions are produced. They are the means by which one actuality enters into the life of another actuality; and they are the bonds of vectorial connectedness between actualities. The concept of the social individual in its most radical meaning is grounded on the notion of constitutive relationships. We live in society, but our society also literally lives within us.

We feed upon each other in all the dimensions of our lives—physically, emotionally, intellectually, spiritually. We create each other. We live within relationships. We live within interlaced fields of energy or relational webs of

---

[14]The fact of becoming is not an emergent. To put it abstractly, becomingness does not itself become. Actual entities become, and there is no becoming apart from the becoming of specific actualities. But there is no reality, actual or otherwise, apart from the fact of becoming. Becoming is coterminous with actuality itself. To be, in the concrete sense, is to become actual. In analogous fashion, relatedness is not an emergent. Various forms of relatedness are historical emergents, but any actuality presupposes the factor of constitutive relatedness.

interconnectedness. Individuals are created within these fields and their possibilities emerge within these interrelationships. This is the reason why I have suggested (on other occasions) that we should commit ourselves to relationships and not to each other, and especially not to the good of the other. In summary, as interrelated individuals we create the web, and the web creates us. Within this relational web we are also self-creative and thereby transform the web—for better or worse.

These considerations add up to the simple yet profound point that as individuals we are interdependent. We do not become interdependent, but rather are such from our inception. This is a primordial fact of our existence. Interdependence or interrelatedness is not an emergent fact. It is indigenous to reality as such, including the realm of possibility as well as the world of actuality.

This point can be extended. We are not interrelated because there is an order in the world. That would be to explain the concrete by the abstract. Rather there is an order because we are interrelated, and this order is an abstraction from the interrelationships. Without interconnectedness there could be no order, unless it were somehow arbitrarily imposed and enforced by an all-powerful and transcendent deity.

Order is a necessary condition in the creation of actualities. It is a condition of limitation, which is a way of saying that it is a principle of actualization. All actualities are finite in that they exclude as well as include. Both inclusion and exclusion occur on the basis of compatibility, whose perimeter includes incompatibility. Since actuality is definable as a process of synthesis, order involves the compatible copresence of contrasting elements whereby a synthesis of them is possible.

The notion of order as compatibility presupposes a reference to specific actualities. Without this reference there would be no basis for incompatibility or exclusion. In the hypothetical situation where everything is equally possible because of the absence of exclusions, the notion of compatibility (and actuality) loses all concrete meaning. Consequently order as abstract harmony is concretized only in the relativities of actual situations.

With respect to specific processes of synthesis, "the compatible copresence of contrasting elements" means that possibilities present themselves as arranged in varying degrees of appropriateness and importance to the emerging purposes of the occasions. (These degrees include those of irrelevance and exclusion.) Order as harmony becomes order as graded relevance (Whitehead).[15]

---

[15]Many interpreters of Whitehead's concept of order as graded relevance understand this to mean that a definite final aim is provided (by God) for each occasion. I think they are mistaken; but if their reading of Whitehead is correct, then I think that Whitehead is in error. The gradation of possibilities is an arrangement of possibilities permissive of the realization of various levels of value or degrees of complexity. It does not furnish us with specific aims. (The aim at the greatest possible value or, more accurately, the greatest value possible, is not a specific aim.) The notion that the order of relevance is quite precisely arranged does not enable us to know concretely which specific elements are most relevant to any specific occasion of experience. Sometimes we cannot know which elements are compatible until they have been synthesized or until the synthesis has been attempted. There are some general limitations. Logical contradiction may constitute one instance. Yet there are emotional, psychic, and spiritual contradictions that can be present (and eventually transformed into compatible contrasts) within a person.

The import of this discussion is that order as graded relevance is a condition that is inherent within the diversity of interconnected elements (in their relations to specific actualities). Order is not an independent or ontologically separable factor that is added to the basic condition of our interconnectedness. Order as a distinguishable factor is analytic in its derivation. Furthermore, the order of relevance of possibilities with respect to any occasion is not arranged by any external agent (God). The shift in relevance of a group of possibilities to different occasions is a function of the complex interplay among all the constituent realities. To think otherwise would seem to deny the principle that the reasons for things are to be found within the things themselves and their relationships to each other.

Still further, we are not interdependent because there is a principle or law of love. This, again, would be to explain the concrete in terms of the abstract. We love because we are interdependent, because we enter into each other's lives.

Love does not create our essential interrelatedness. Love is an acknowledgment of it. We love because we are bound to each other, because we live and are fulfilled in, with, and through each other. We love because a failure to love is a denial of the other, ourselves, and our relatedness. It results in a diminution of all of us, including God. We respond to the suffering of another because he is another and because he is suffering, but this does not tell the whole story. When we reach out toward the other in sympathy or compassion or love, we acknowledge our oneness with the other. His suffering becomes in part our suffering; his impoverishment diminishes us. Our response becomes his resource. In responding appropriately to the other we are both fulfilled through that act, and life within the web of relationships is advanced. All the religious virtues are virtues of relationships.

Love (which some refer to as a law of life) is obligatory because we are members one of another and because we are all members of the web of interconnectedness within which we all live. Without our interdependence within this web, love would not be obligatory. The notion that we are to love God and each other because God loves us has force only because our lives are bound up with each other and with God, and because His life is bound up with ours. The parable of the Last Judgment is the text for this point.

In short, love does not create the world; it recreates and redeems it. Love (except as a principle of harmony or compatibility) does not cause the world to cohere in one unity; it adds a richness and tragic beauty to the given unity. The unity is inherent within the matrix of interrelated entities, both those that are possible and those that are actual. The unity and the interrelatedness of things are exemplified as much in the mutual destructiveness of evil as they are in the mutual enrichment of a loving relationship. Love does not create the societal character of the web; it transforms the society of the web into a concerned community.

Love is not a substance. It is a quality of energy whereby external relations, or relations of indifference and bare toleration, may be transformed into internal relationships, and internal relationships may be deepened and enhanced.

The notion of our interrelatedness or interdependence is surely one of the basic insights of the biblical understanding of life. This understanding was expressed in terms of covenantal relationships and the concept of the kingdom of God. Covenants in the biblical sense involved relationships between God and a people. The interrelatedness of the members of the community did not clearly entail an interdependence between God and the people, although there was a unilateral dependence of the people on God. Within biblical understanding there seems to be a limitation to the range of the notion of interdependence, a limitation that is not present in my own theologizing. Yet within these limits there is some similarity between the biblical understanding of covenantal relationships and what I call the relational web of life.

The Bible has different meanings for various people. One of its most important functions consists in its being a record of the tortuous evolution in a people's understanding of the nature and the meaning of the basic divine-human covenantal relationship. This evolution and this tradition culminated in the person of Jesus, whose life, work, and teaching (according to the early church) were of such stature that the heights and depths of the meaning of the covenant had been made known; the heart of God and the spirit of man had been revealed; and both man and God were defined in terms of their involvement in the web of the convenantal kingdom. The relational life, or the interdependent life of the kingdom, was envisioned and embodied. The cross and resurrection set forth both the price and the recreative power of this kind of life—for God and man alike. Most of us reject the relational life within the interdependent web much of the time. In the midst of our several inequalities we are all equally dependent upon the life within the web.

The Bible is also an extraordinary record of the many ways that we resist, deny, and reject the existence and meaning of this web, this interdependence, this relational life of the cross and resurrection. The themes of this resistance have resounded through centuries of church history. Most of them involve a failure to acknowledge and accept the fulfillment of life that comes through grace, which is a gift of the relational life. In this respect the evolutionary struggle recorded within the Bible is recapitulated in each of us.

It should be added that the Bible is one record of the evolution in the creation of specific webs of interrelationship, creations that more fully exemplified the fulfillment that is possible within the interdependence that lies at the foundations of our existence.

We all live in various webs of interrelatedness, some smaller, some larger. As a consequence of Jesus and the revelatory founders of other religions, we have come to see that the stature of our humanity is in large part a function of the inclusiveness of the communal web in which we feel at home—an insight that G. H. Mead has spelled out in terms of his behavioral psychology. We have come to understand that at the human level the web of life includes all humankind. This all-inclusive human web is the primordial convenant—primordial in the sense of being coterminous with human life—to which all are called and all are chosen, and in whose service all covenants of lesser generality, both religious and secular, receive their justification.

We are slowly, perhaps too slowly, coming to understand that the human community belongs to a larger web that includes all forms of terrestrial life. In certain respects we transcend the world of nature, although these differences may be distinctions of degree and not of kind. Nevertheless, our transcendence establishes neither our independence of nature nor our imperial status in the scheme of things. Our freedom as individuals emerges from our relationships. We are related in order to be free—that is, we are related in order to fulfill ourselves as individuals. It is also (and more profoundly) the case that we are free in order to establish deeper and more far-reaching relationships. We achieve our greatest fulfillment not in, by, and for ourselves, but in terms of those finer relationships we help to create and by which we are sustained. When we use our freedom to deny our interdependence with others, including the world of nature, we also assume the prerogative to try to control nature and use it for our own autonomous purposes. When we act as though man is the measure, then we not only befoul our own nest; we shred the web and impoverish all life. The web is not only the context of our lives; it is the measure of all life.

Our identities as individual persons may derive in part from our transcendence of nature and of other people. But, the basic organismic orientation upon which our personal identity is dependent is a function of the complex interplay of the motions of the celestial bodies that make up our solar system. Unless our bodies are attuned to the motions of these spheres, we would have no directional center. We would not know where or who we are. We are not only distant relatives of the nonhuman members of the spaceship earth; we are quite literally creations of the transcendent firmament. The evolution of our planetary life is not only a fantastic tale of the incredible and cunning creativity of life's powers exhibited over vast stretches of time; it is equally an awesome and humbling story of the "enormous interlinked complexity of life" as Loren Eiseley made the point by citing the poet Francis Thompson: "One could not pluck a flower without troubling a star."

These human and planetary webs of interconnectedness are functions of creative and dynamic relationships. If the foundational elements and conditions of our world were not given as interlaced and interdependent, there would be no way to create this basic interdependence. When, in our openness and by our efforts, we establish webs of relationships, we are not uniting fundamental factors that previously were radically disjoined. We are rather exemplifying and extending the interrelatedness that is a given condition of our lives and of all life.

This interconnectedness is not simply one fact among many other equally significant facts. It is a preeminent fact. It is a condition that is presupposed in every experience of personal wholeness and socialized existence. When interconnectedness is conjoined with the process of becoming, we have arrived at the elemental matrix of life and existence in any form. This matrix is the elemental shape of social life and the creative context within which individual life is actualized.

We are led ineluctably to extend the range of application of the concept of the web. The widest generalization of the notion of interdependence results in the proposition that the world, in the most inclusive sense, is an indefinitely extended field of interconnected events. The term *indefinitely* indicates that the limits of this extended web cannot be established. One can say that the concept of this extended web is a generalization of field theory, or the utmost expansion of our sense of community. Or, I suggest that it can be interpreted as an imaginative extension of the sentence: "Inasmuch as you have done it unto one of the least of these, you have done it unto me."

The Unity of the Web

The idea of the world as in some sense one world, one unified whole, does involve an imaginative leap of some magnitude. It is a far-flung generalization and admittedly this idea is a vague notion. The attempt to give it definite empirical content would take us beyond the limits of scientific evidence. Yet the basis upon which the generalization is grounded does have some support in scientific theory. Some empirical evidence may also be derived from more concrete forms of experience than those employed in strictly scientific enterprises. The vision of the unity of human life, and of all life, is an ancient concept growing out of prolonged inquiry. This theme has rootage in poetic insight, parapsychological phenomena, and in deep intuitions emanating from several religious traditions, including those of the American Indians.

The introduction of the notion of religious intuitions into the empirical tradition of process-relational modes of thought raises a host of problems. Most of these center on the question of evidence and the limits of evidence. Evidence is a function of perception (and accessible data), and perception is a matter of sensitive discernment. Discernment is a variable, reflecting the inequality of sensitivity among observers. In order to obtain a discerning and penetrating "seeing," physical perception must be informed and prepared by appropriate and suggestive theory that guides our seeing, prefigures possible connections, and enlarges our receptivity concerning what may be presented to us. (It should be noted that it is also the case that physical experience guides, corrects, and enlarges our conceptual receptivity.) Because of this interplay between the physical and conceptual dimensions of our experience, perception is not a bare and wholly innocent seeing. It is an interpreted seeing, an understanding. This understanding has its meaning and truth-status only within a more inclusive background of interconnected meaning, even if this larger framework is only presupposed.

The final aim, as Whitehead suggests, may be the achievement of self-evidence. But with respect to the issues that concern us most profoundly, decisive and persuasive evidence (not to mention self-evidence) is not easily or quickly obtainable.

The testimony of fundamental religious intuitions derives from a sensitivity to qualities and relationships of more than usual depth and range. These intuitions seem to be constituted by a very close integration of physical and conceptual feelings exemplifying wide generality of import. The generality of interconnectedness is experienced physically and conceptually.

It would seem to be the case that religious intuitions, however profound and penetrating, do not take us beyond the fundamental conditions of our known world. Within this cosmological limitation, the descriptive range and power of these intuitions, and the status of descriptive generalizations based upon them, are at least unclear.

These methodological questions (which are merely outlined here) arise because of the thesis of this essay, which identifies God and the world. This thesis grows out of a devotion to the concrete nature of God, which, in turn, is grounded in a conviction concerning the inadequacy of an abstract God. These methodological problems may prove to be insurmountable, and this version of an empirical stance within this (or any other) mode of thought may be felt by many to be inadequate, theologically and religiously. However, the alternative approaches within the process-relational outlook also have their problematic aspects. These alternatives can be briefly noted.

First, at least some of the methodological problems associated with an empirical approach to the notion of the unity of the world (and to the concreteness of God) can be transcended by an a priori method. Charles Hartshorne, for example, contends that a contingent God arrived at by an empirical method is not worthy of our worship;

only a God who exists necessarily merits devotion. By means of a reconstructed ontological argument that is premised on a conception of perfection which is illustrated in Whitehead's concrete/abstract God, Hartshorne concludes that this God exists in the mode of necessity. Since this God is concrete, with an unchanging abstract character, it follows that some concrete state of God (or some concrete world) must exist or be actualized. This actualized state is the actual world in which we live. It is God's body, and as such it is a concrete unity. It is contingent in its mode of existence since it could have been otherwise. God is therefore actual as an incredibly complex and living subject (or personal society) with an unambiguous character.

Hartshorne concedes that the ontological argument is valid only on the basis of a conception of God akin to Whitehead's. On any other premise the argument is invalid; that is, it results in self-contradiction. Furthermore, the world makes sense only in terms of the kind of God who exemplifies the qualities and performs the functions entailed in the notion of perfection that is the premise of the argument (such as the perfect preservation of all actualized values). Apart from this kind of God life is meaningless. So both ontological necessity and the meaningfulness of life are grounded on an idea, a meaning. This idea has empirical rootage, but its a priori character and validity derive from the claims of abstract logic.

The premodern philosophers of substance (or being) who devised the ontological argument apparently believed that their value premises established the validity of the argument. Philosophers of process (and others) believe they have shown that the argument, based on the premises of substance thought, is invalid. Hartshorne believes that the inadequacies of substance premises have been overcome by the premise of process-relational modes of thought and that the validity of the argument has been thereby assured.

But are these premises beyond criticism? Even if we assume that there is some philosophical and theological advance in the history of these inquiries in the West, this advance has occurred within the evolution of Western thought and experience. Are we to assume that this evolution has reached its zenith? The logic of ontological necessity appears to be, at least in some respects, a device to assert the unsurpassability of our historically achieved value insights.

In terms of Western experience, in what sense is the encounter of ancient Israel with the figure of Jesus paradigmatic? The Jews had their understanding of God's convenant with them. They awaited the coming of a messiah who would confirm and actualize their deepest meanings and expectations. For them, any alternative conception was a spiritual self-contradiction and a denial of life's meaningfulness. For them, the coming of a messiah shaped in the image of their expectations and value judgments was their "ontological necessity." But, from a Christian perspective, the messiah who came was not the messiah who was expected.

On what self-evident grounds are we philosophically and theologically invulnerable to an encounter with an unexpected messiah? In terms of what irrefutable considerations are we privileged to believe that the self-transcending restiveness inherent within revelatory events and figures has been once and for all overcome by one particular revelation, or by the emergence of a philosophic perspective such as process philosophy?

Beyond this caveat concerning the historical relativity of the value premises upon which the ontological argument is grounded, there is another consideration. The stipulated perfection and unambiguousness of God's unchanging character is, in fact, a conception of God's character. But God's actual character does not correspond to this conception. The next section of this essay will contend that there are no unambiguous, concrete actualities in the world of our experience. God as concretely actual is involved in ambiguity. In Hartshorne's system God's character can be analytically abstracted from His actuality; but the character of God that is abstracted is not unambiguous. An unambiguous structure or character can be derived only by a complex abstractive process, the end result of which has no counterpart in reality. In short, the conception of the character of God that constitutes the premise of the ontological argument, which ostensibly establishes the necessary existence of God, is not the character of the God who is concretely actual.

The philosophy of a priori necessity is or tends to be a philosophy of abstractions. The religious stance of a theology of God's necessary existence harbors the impulse to become the worship of an idea of God. It acknowledges the reality of mystery, but it subsumes its sense of mystery under the structures of its metaphysics. The empirical philosophy of attachment attempts to think and live in terms of holding its ascertained structures of experience subject to the dynamic presence of mystery.

There is a second alternative that defines the unity of the world abstractly in terms of a universal order. God is then identified as the abstract source or principle of this order. This option is illustrated in Whitehead's conception of the primordial or abstract nature of God—a conception that is adopted by many of Whitehead's disciples. As we saw previously, in Whitehead's system order is a gradation of relevance among diverse possibilities in relation to any concrete occasion of experience. This gradation is required if the process of actualization is to result in the creation of definite or limited actuality. These possibilities include novel forms. These possibilities and their relevance change in accordance with different personal, social, and historical contexts, but the pattern of graded relevance remains fixed. As the principle of order, God is the principle of concretion.

Within this interpretation some Whiteheadians associate God primarily with the future. In this respect God functions as the abstract ground for hope.

A principle of order may have a wider and deeper status in the scheme of things than an ideal.[16] God conceived as a principle of order does all that an abstraction can do. But the net effect of this alternative is to reduce God to a final cause whose aim is not basically distinguishable from the best of historically relative, human ideals. Human ideals also function as lures to their actualization in due season. They may also embody the principle of self-transcendence with respect to creative novelty. They can be an adequate basis for "the adventure of ideas." Beyond this, the commitment to a transcending principle of order, even with its persuasive appeal for an openness to forms of creative novelty conceptually envisaged as relevant ideal aims, can be as idolatrous and destructive as the commitment to projected humanistic ideals. The in-

---

[16]The reader is referred to the previous discussion of order, 32-33.

adequacies of a religious life oriented to abstractions—be they ideas, forms, ideals, possibilities, or an order—are not overcome by calling these abstractions divine.

An emphasis on the ultimacy of process has or could have a significant religious consequence. It should enable us to be more alert to the distinction between the actuality of God and our ideas about God. The actuality of God is dynamic process. Our ideas are forms of symbols. Ideas are indispensable to our living as humans, but they are not the proper objects of an adequate religious commitment. We do not need to be philosophic instrumentalists with respect to the status of ideas or symbols in order to maintain that they exist for the sake of the enhancement of actuality and our relation to it. Symbols may guide our commitment, but even this guidance is subservient to the working of the process of actuality.

There is the fact of process and there is process as a concept. There is a process of creative transformation and there is transformation as an idea to be realized. The two are by no means the same. Our commitment to this *process* of transformation is not to be equated with a commitment to transformation as such, or to transformation as an idea if this gets translated into being an openness to some relevant conceptual novelty. Conceptual openness has its high importance, but as a form of commitment it is a devotion to abstractions. As a type of religious commitment it exemplifies the "fallacy of misplaced concreteness."

It is, of course, the case that within the Whiteheadian system God is also concrete. This means that God is actual as an incredibly complex process wherein the activities of the actual world are internalized and synthesized into the unity of an experiential subject of experience. As a consequence of this process the actual world becomes an organismic unity within the concrete actuality of God (panentheism).

There would seem to be two alternative routes by which to attempt to establish the concrete actuality of Whitehead's God. (Whitehead himself is less than precise about the method he employs.) One route is rationalistic, and the other is empirical. The rationalistic alternative would involve some such method as Hartshorne's ontological argument, a point of view we have discussed above.

Empirically, there is the primacy of the principle that the concreteness of actuality is neither derivable from, nor explainable by, the abstract. This means that the presumed fact of the abstract unity of the world does not in itself entail the concrete unity of the world. Stated alternatively, it means that the abstract reality of God (viewed as a principle of order) does not in itself establish His concrete reality. We can "move" from the abstract reality of God as order to the actuality of God as the concrete unity of the world only if we understand order to be an abstraction from the presupposed interconnectedness of events.

The evidence that is relevant to Whitehead's conception of God would seem to be derived from the interconnectedness of events and the qualities experienced in profound religious intuitions. It is quite problematic whether this evidence is sufficient to establish the concrete actuality of God as an experiencing subject.

On the assumption that Whitehead's method is that of speculative empiricism rather than that of the rational a priori, it may be the case that with regard to their adoption of the concrete nature of God many Whiteheadians are, at least implicitly, Hartshornians.

Third, there is another empirical theological alternative to the one I am proposing. Although its focus is on the conception of God as a concrete and creative actuality, it is not concerned with the problem of the concrete unity of the world. Since
the actual world manifests a diversity of forces, many of which are either noncreative
or destructive in nature, God is identified with one aspect of the world or one kind
of process. This is the process of creative transformation. This creative process exhibits an unchanging character whereby this kind of process is distinguishable from
all other processes. This character is understood to be unambiguous.

In the following section it will be suggested that a God that is identified with an
aspect of the world (e.g., Wieman's fourfold creative process) is an abstract and not
a concrete God.[17]

To return to the question of the nature of the unity of the indefinitely extended
web of interconnected events, three conceptions seem to be most relevant to our inquiry. First, there is the unity of an occasion of experience. This organic unity is that
of an experiencing subject in the immediacy of its becoming. The unity, like the occasion itself, is momentary in its duration.

Second, there is the unity of an event. This can be defined both concretely and
abstractly. Concretely, the unity of an event constitutes a historic route of successive
occasions, but the route itself is not an occasion. The abstract unity can be understood
as a recurring structure that characterizes the enduring object in its persistence
throughout the duration of the inclusive event.

Third, there is the unity of a nexus and a society. The concrete unity of both consists in the genetic interrelatedness of the members of the enduring group. The difference between them is that the unity of a society may also be defined abstractly in
terms of a shared manner of feeling and action, a common character or ethos.

The nature of the unity of the web would seem to lie between two extremes. On
the one extreme the world as a whole does not appear empirically to have the unity
of an experiencing subject, conceived as an unimaginably complex process of subjective synthesis. Certain religious intuitions may modify the stark simplicity of this
conclusion, although intuitions of the unity of the actual world may not provide evi-

---

[17]Another and quite different suggestion could be mentioned. There is the conception of a plenum, or
a fullness, which has the unity of a continuum. This is an ancient theory going back at least as far as Plato's
receptacle. Whitehead has revitalized this notion in terms of his concept of the extensive continuum. It is
clear that for Whitehead extensive connectedness, as a factor in the construction of the world, is not first
introduced by the process of actualization. It is also found at the level of possibility in his system. But
extensiveness, or extensive connection, as a continuum is a characteristic of potentiality and not of actuality. Actuality, as Whitehead insists, is incurably atomic. Thus the extensive connectedness of actuality
cannot take the form of a continuum. The connectedness within actuality can be exemplified within a web
of relationships involving particular actualities that are in some sense discontinuous, even though they are
related through their causal connection. The web of relationships constitutes the extensive field. In Whitehead's system this extensive field of concrete actualities exists within the larger and more inclusive extensive continuum of abstract potentiality. Furthermore, this extensive field is not a web of material objects.
It is a field of interconnected events. Concrete interconnectedness, like relativity, is found only between
events and not between material objects. The point was made previously that material objects—such as
chairs, trees, and people—exist as recurring or persistent structures only within the relativistic contexts of
interconnected events or enduring societies of events.

dence of this particular kind of subjective unity. (If the world does not have the unity of an occasion, then it cannot have the unity of an event.)

On the other extreme, the world seems to be something more than an aggregated totality. To be sure, in certain respects the unity of the world may appear to be rather loose and indeterminate. But, the general order of things would seem to attest to a unity that has more structure and cohesiveness than are involved in a vast conglomerate whose components basically exemplify external relationships.

The tentative conclusion of this oversimplified analysis is that this universal web of interconnected events has the kind of unity the term ''web'' suggests, namely, that of a generalized enduring society. The fundamental characteristics of this society (which make it a society rather than a nexus or a totality of nexus) are definable only in terms of the utmost universality because it ''includes'' all other societies of lesser generality as well as all occasions and events. These characteristics would probably consist of certain elemental properties of extensive connection.

It should be emphasized that this societal web is not a ''society with a personal order'' or a ''person'' in the Whiteheadian sense. It is much more akin to Whitehead's description of the world of nature as an ''organic extensive community . . . that is always passing beyond itself.''[18]

In terms of this analysis, God as a wholeness is to be identified with the concrete, interconnected totality of this struggling, imperfect, unfinished, and evolving societal web. As this universal society God includes all modes of temporality; God also operates through all the Aristotelian causes. God's action is not wholly or even primarily identified with the persuasive and permissive lure of a final cause or a relevant and novel ideal, as is the case in Whiteheadian thought. An exclusive or even a primary emphasis on final causation is abstractionism. God is also physical, efficient cause that may be either creative or inertial in its effects.

Stated otherwise, God is not only, or perhaps even primarily, the divine eros, understood as a conceptual appetition toward the good. This, again, is an abstract mode of operation that has its important role; but more concretely, God is expressed as the organic restlessness of the whole body of creation, as this drive is unequally exemplified in the several parts of this societal web. This discontent, which is an expression of the essential ''spirit'' of any creature, may exemplify itself as an expansive urge toward greater good. It may also become a passion for greater evil that, however disguised or rationalized as a greater good, also has its attractiveness.

Furthermore, God is not only the ultimate end for which all things exist; God is also the shape and stuff of existence.

These points of emphasis are to be understood in the context of the self-creativity and relative independence of individual creatures who yet have their being only in community.

All of this having been said, the question naturally arises: Why deify this interconnected web of existence by calling it ''God''? Why not simply refer to the world and to the processes of life? Since, in terms of this perspective, the being of God is not other than the being of the world; since to speak of God is to refer to the world

---

[18] Whitehead, *Process and Reality,* 289.

in some sense; and more decisively, since God is not an enduring concrete individual with a sustained subjective life, what is gained by this perhaps confusing, semantic identification?

The justification for the identification is both ontological and pragmatic in the deepest Jamesian sense. In our traditions the term "God" is the symbol of ultimate values and meanings in all of their dimensions. It connotes an absolute claim on our loyalty. It bespeaks a primacy of trust, and a priority within the ordering of our commitments. It points the direction of a greatness of fulfillment. It signifies a richness of resources for the living of life at its depths. It suggests the enshrinement of our common and ecological life. It proclaims an adequate object of worship. It symbolizes a transcendent and inexhaustible meaning that forever eludes our grasp.

The world is God because it is the source and preserver of meaning; because the creative advance of the world in its adventure is the supreme cause to be served; because even in our desecration of our space and time within it, the world is holy ground; and because it contains and yet enshrouds the ultimate mystery inherent within existence itself. "God" symbolizes this incredible mystery. The existent world embodies it. The world in all the dimensions of its being is the basis for all our wonder, awe, and inquiry.

Yet the question persists. The world, conceived as this universal web, includes all the evil, wastes, destructiveness, regressions, ugliness, horror, disorder, complacency, dullness, and meaninglessness, as well as their opposites. Why then choose the relational life of the cross, or the discipline of the artist, or any other form of life that requires sensitivity, suffering, fidelity, trust, openness, and creative labor? Since all is in God, why not opt for a life engrossed in the several levels and dimensions of self-gratification, or the subtler and more demonic forms of destructiveness—in short, a life dedicated to the actualization of nothingness? Since the interdependence of life is as well illustrated in mutual destruction as in the relational life of the cross, why choose the cross? Why not choose hell?

The answer lies in comparing the level of stature that is available under each choice. It is a matter of evidence. With respect to the deepest questions, the search for evidence becomes the quest for self-evidence. The ultimate manifestation of self-evidence occurs at the level of embodied valuations. And stature, wherever found, is the most impregnable and incontrovertible form of self-evidence. Beyond it there is no court of appeal. On this hangs all the law and the prophets—and all the revelations.

In this web of interrelatedness there are aims and purposes almost beyond measure. Some are compatible, some are cooperative, and others are mutually enhancing. Others are contraries, and still others are mutually contradictory and destructive. In and through, because of, and in spite of this diversity and these contradictions and this disorder, there persists a restlessness or a tropism not only to live, but to live well and to live better (Whitehead).[19] This passion carries its own appeal, its own authority and warrant, and its own limited strength to fulfill itself in due season.

---

[19]Alfred North Whitehead, *The Function of Reason* (Boston: Beacon Press, 1959) 8.

But this passion for greater life and stature does not exist apart from all other passions that aim at or result in the actualization of smaller stature. It participates in them and they in it. Thus we are led to our third topic.

The Ambiguity Within God

Years ago Reinhold Niebuhr contended that Christian faith could not be expressed adequately in terms of a naturalistic philosophy because every natural and historical process is ambiguous in character. Niebuhr's implicit premise is that Christian faith is rooted in the idea of perfection. The thesis of this section accepts Niebuhr's observation concerning the ineradicable presence of ambiguity, but denies the actuality of (and the need for) the unambiguous. On the contrary, the thesis asserts that the unambiguous has at best the status of an abstraction, and that consequently an ambiguous God is of greater stature than an unambiguous deity.

The point involved may be misunderstood. The aim in the first instance is not to seek and cherish ambiguity for its own sake. The aim is qualitative richness. The quest in the first instance is not for an ambiguous God. The quest is for a living, dynamic, and active God—in short, a concrete God. An ambiguous God is not of greater stature simply because He is ambiguous. His greater size derives from the concreteness of His actuality in contrast to the reality of a nonliving, undynamic, and inactive abstraction. The concretely actual is ambiguous; only the highly abstract can be unambiguous. Thus, the conclusion, and the thesis, that an ambiguous God is of greater stature than an unambiguous deity.

In its conception of God, Christian theology has been obsessed with God as embodied perfection. From its beginning down to the present, theology has taken it as axiomatic that God is unambiguous in character. (In this tradition only the unambiguous can be perfect. Or, conversely, only the perfect is unambiguous.) God's goodness has been conceived as pure and unmixed, the personification of unambiguous love.

The Christologies of the church, by and large, reflect this same passion for perfection. Jesus Christ, as the unexcelled representative and the unsurpassable historical embodiment of God's perfect love for the world, has also been conceived as unambiguous in His being, sinless and completely at one with the divine purity. The unambiguity of God could be symbolized adequately only by another unambiguous figure.[20]

There seems to be some internal relationship between the traditional view of the unambiguous character of God and the notion that the being of God is independent of the being of the world. The precise nature of this relationship is not decisive for our purposes, but surely without the latter notion the former is difficult, if not impossible, to maintain. In any case, the ontological transcendence of the God of tradition means that God is not of the world. Yet this God acts in the world. He makes Himself known through his activity, or at least through the results of His activity,

---

[20]It is interesting to note that the crucifixion of Jesus was the basic (or perhaps the only) example of unambiguous love that Niebuhr found in the world.

such as the creation and sustained existence of the world, and the redemption of lost souls. As the unity of perfect wisdom and sovereign power, God is responsible for having established the basic structure of the world, the fundamental conditions of natural and historical existence. The traditional doctrine of the goodness of creation (which is often employed in discussions concerning the nature of sin and evil) seems to imply that the basic structure of the world is unambiguously good. If this is the case, then not only the evil but also the ambiguity in the world derive from the misuse of these conditions by the creatures, especially the human species. On the other hand, if ambiguity were shown to be an inherent characteristic of the created world, then the God of tradition could be defined as ambiguous, at least as judged by the foundational conditions resulting from His creative activity.

Theologians as well as other Western thinkers have noticed, of course, that the world of our experience is at odds with itself. With differing degrees of decisiveness they have recognized that our world, especially at the human level, is filled with evil and ambiguous elements that thwart and bedevil the noblest purposes of God and man. Now whether these factors are inherent within the structure of the world, or are due to creaturely sin and evil or to the presence of demonic powers, they have been interpreted in the tradition as being finally phenomenal in nature. That is, they are not characteristics of ultimate reality. For these thinkers the very meaning of *meaning* is wholly dependent on the eventual or ultimate overcoming of these problematic conditions. Unless this general resolution occurs (in one way or another) life has no basic or intrinsic meaning.

Consequently these thinkers have concluded that the final answer to the ambiguity and evil in the world lies either in an unambiguous and perfected God, or in a transcendental realm that is the domain of a perfected and indivisible whole. The answer is variously phrased, but the responses are analogous. They are in fact variations on a theme. In one mode of thought after another it has been maintained that ultimately the partial and fragmentary meanings we achieve will be completed; phenomenal appearances in all dimensions of life will give way to God-perceived reality; the obscure will be clarified; the ambiguous will be purified; the contradictions of life will be resolved; and sin and evil will be vanquished by a triumphant goodness.

This general principle can be briefly illustrated. For Reinhold Niebuhr the unambiguous and sacrificial love of Jesus Christ (on the cross) must be vindicated if life is to be affirmed as meaningful. It must ''pay off'' in terms of historical consequences. However, the actual course of human history is a refutation of the power of sacrificial love. The sacrifice has not paid off and the vindication has not occurred. Thus, viewed in terms of history, the world in itself has no intrinsic meaning. Therefore in Niebuhr's thought there must be a ''point beyond history'' where this justification takes place.

For Kant the fulfillment of the moral imperative should be conjoined with the realization of human happiness if life is to make sense. In actual life this union, the *summum bonum,* does not occur. Therefore there must be an immortality wherein this unambiguous and complete union is realized. (Immortality is also the condition wherein the limitations of phenomenal understanding are transcended.)

The dominant tradition of Western thought has proceeded on the value premise that the resolution of the ambiguous, in terms of the perfect and unambiguous, is a development from the less to the more. The thesis of this section asserts that the converse is the case, that this movement is a transition from the more to the less. In terms of the language and outlook of this essay, it is a movement from the concrete to the abstract. From this perspective, the traditional resolution of the ambiguity of life is an abstract justification of a theoretical vindication. This is to say that it is not a resolution. The tragic richness of the concretely actual can never be redeemed by the poverty of abstractions, however purified they may be.

In process-relational modes of thought the being of God is not independent of the being of the world. Thus whatever unambiguity may be ascribed to God in this way of looking at things, this quality cannot derive from God's ontological transcendence. Yet some representatives of this philosophy seek an unambiguous God. They are concerned with transcending the ambiguity of the world. They, too, believe that the answer to ambiguity is to be found within the unambiguous. They attempt to do this by one or another type of abstraction. An evaluation of these efforts can be facilitated by a discussion of the nature of ambiguity.

Ambiguities derive from the basic characteristics of individuals and societies. They emerge out of the dynamic and relational features of experience.

Ambiguities arise in the first place because of the composite nature of individuals as occasions of experience. (The composite character of occasions is due to the immanence of several causal influences in the becoming of an individual.) The several components within an individual are interrelated. In becoming something definite an individual makes a decision, or emerges as a decision. The decision is single, but it need not be single-minded. The unity of individuality often includes the presence of tension or incompatibility between the internalized causal influences. Each influence makes its claim and has its own appeal. In his composite unity an individual may be pulled in several directions. His motives may be mixed, causing him to be at odds with himself. His "decision" may embrace various indecisions and irresolutions. Possibilities may be ordered in their relevance for an individual (as Whitehead believes), but this hierarchical presentation may not be matched by a corresponding order of priorities within the subjective life of that individual.

In the second place, this point may be extended in terms of the interconnected character of enduring individuals. As we have seen previously, individuals participate in each other. This mutual participation defines the way that environing society lives within the individual. This entails the consequence that an individual cannot fully determine the quality of his life by himself, by a resolution of his will, however enlightened and decently motivated he may be. The confusions, prejudices, contradictions, and brokenness of his society are present as shaping forces within him. He may mitigate their power, but he cannot be completely free from their influence until they are eliminated from his world. From this point of view, the notion of a sinless and unambiguous savior existing within a sinful society is an impossibility.

Third, the dynamics of life are such that ambiguity seems to be almost a built-in quality of the elemental processes of creation. The relationships and institutions that bring us into being and shape us are the same forces that tend to restrict us to conformal patterns of thought and behavior and thereby to minimize our freedom. Society is one of the sources of our freedom. The health of a society requires the relative autonomy of its members. Yet there is something in the very nature of a society that is antithetical to the exercise of freedom by its citizens.

The strength that is poured into the formation of our virtues is the same strength that overplays itself and tempts us to think and act as though our virtues were more inclusive and adequate than they are: In this fashion our virtues become vices and our strengths, weaknesses. This consequence is a function of the expansive and self-centered character of spirit. The individual does not come equipped with a self-regulator by which his appropriate limitations are determined and maintained.

The passion that compels us to search for truth is the same drive that leads to our neuroses and defensiveness when the truth (especially about ourselves) is more than we feel we can or want to bear. The repressions that function as "normal self-protection and creative self-restriction" (Becker)[21] can easily lead to destructive neuroses and result in a refusal to enter a wider life.

The energy that is shaped by the disciplines of our intellectual and vocational specializations whereby we acquire greater knowledge and competence is the same energy that develops inertial qualities that blunt our sensitivities to other dimensions and perspectives of experience. The structures that are essential to the realization of specific and definite actualities also tend to staticize the very forms of life they made possible.

Fourth, the dialectic of life breeds its own ambiguities. The spirit moves toward creative freedom, but it becomes institutionalized because spirit must assume specific forms. Institutions are the means whereby the spirit becomes socialized. However, in this very process institutions tend to domesticate and stultify the spirit.

The individual is dependent upon his relationships for his very being; he is an emergent from them. Yet the very achievement of his individuality tempts him to deny his essential dependence and to make himself the center of his own existence.

The moment of success in any advance seems to create two contrasting impulses. On the one hand there is a restlessness to continue the advance to a more complex stage, even though this effort requires a finer and more demanding discipline. On the other hand there is an impulse to rest and to be content with the good that has been achieved. This leads to fixation and defensiveness. The strength and devotion that caused us to labor and sacrifice to achieve a goal is the same energy that leads us to cling to the plateau of our achievement. The energy of success may become entropic in that it moves in the direction of creating a closed system. In this manner success may become the enemy of further creative advance, and the good becomes the foe of the better. The adage is confirmed that "to travel hopefully is better than to arrive."

Reinhold Niebuhr's reiterated insight, that every advance in goodness brings with it the possibility of greater evil, entails the caveat that there is no progressive conquest of evil. On the contrary, the forms of destruction or diminution take on a character and a strength that are proportional to the character and strength of the advance. In this fashion every creative advance may give rise to its contrary or to some condition that either negates or qualifies the advance.

---

[21]Ernest Becker, *The Denial of Death* (New York: The Free Press, 1973) 178.

Within the movement of this dialectic not only do various gains entail some loss, but in many instances the higher levels of achievement become increasingly fragile in their constitution. They become more vulnerable to destructive and disintegrating forces. Greater vigilance, finer sensitivity, and more energy are required for their survival. In democratic societies, an insistent openness to contrasting points of view, a sensitive regard for the rights of all, a knowing commitment to the common good in the face of countless pressure groups, and a firm resolve to maintain a judicious and viable structure of checks and balances—these great, fragile, and hard-won values are easily forgotten, ignored, or trampled on by the callous and the unknowing. In the arena of sports, it is much more difficult to remain a champion than to become one.

It is true that some good may emerge from the ashes of destructive evil, although too often it requires a catastrophic event to bestir us sufficiently to take any constructive action. It is of course also true that qualities of goodness may be transformed into demonic attributes; but it is easier to transform goodness into evil than to transmute evil into goodness. It is easier to arrest the advance of goodness than to block the inertia of evil. To repeat an earlier characterization concerning the energy of success, evil, in contrast to creative goodness, moves in the direction of creating a closed system. Evil thereby tends to become entropic.

Fifth, the ambivalence of life, at least at the human level, is found at the core of the human spirit. On the other hand we are fearful of failure, anxious to realize our potentialities. We want the most of what life has to offer. We say that we yearn for the fullness of experience. But on the other hand we are also fearful of success. We draw back not only from the cost of success, the courage and discipline required to achieve our highest potential. We retreat also from the obligations, the challenges, and the risks that follow high achievement. The fullness of life is too much. We are afraid to die, and we are afraid to live deeply and with great openness. We would avoid the seeming nothingness of death, and yet the fullness of life seems to be too big and unmanageable. Its price is too great. We desire to be our own unique selves, and yet we want the comfort and safety of anonymity.

It may be the case, as Becker claims, that we cannot face the full truth of life in an open and unprotected manner and live. It may be that the truth is such that life in its rawness is unmanageable, and that we must live in terms of various defense mechanisms (or what Becker calls "lies") whereby life is reduced to manageable proportions. If this is so, then our psychic and spiritual ambiguities may function as forms of protection that make life possible for many or most of us.

Lastly, the pervasiveness of ambiguity may be seen in contemplating the goodness and evil of a person. We cannot divide the seamless cloth of actuality, especially the concrete actuality of the self. There are no separable or autonomous divisions within the self. There is no part of the self that is the fountainhead of goodness and another part that is the ground of evil. Virtues and vices, while distinguishable in their natures, are inseparable with respect to their source. The good and evil of a person derive from the same origin. They are in fact two sides of one coin. This common source is the basic spirit of the individual. The spirit, which is the unity of the self in its self-creative freedom, includes all the forms of ambiguity we have discussed above.

The specific qualities and dimensions of an individual's goodness reflect the qualities and dimensions of his spirit. These features embrace all the interdependent facets of his personality and character, including his capacity for evil. The qualities of goodness are inseparable from these diverse elements. This ambiguous and composite goodness, which arises out of the ambiguity and the dimensions of his spirit, is the only concrete goodness he possesses. He has no other goodness.

This seamless actuality of the self houses the composite unity of the spirit of an individual. Within this unity of the spirit the inseparability of the capacities for good and evil is rooted. This means that the evil of a person cannot be exorcised without decimating his capacity for achieving goodness. The evil proclivities of a person can be transmuted only by transforming his essential spirit. This entails the proposition that the tradition's conception of love, which has the quality of "in spite of," must be transcended. A love that is truly adequate has no qualifications of acceptance, rare as this kind of love is. If, as some psychologists insist, there is no light and good "side" of the self without the presence of a dark shadow, then the whole person must be accepted if the creative advance of life is to be enhanced.

With this discussion of ambiguity as background, we now return to the topic of the propensity of process-relational thinkers to search for the unambiguous. This will be carried out in terms of an evaluation of the work of Whitehead and Wieman.

Henry Nelson Wieman's underlying concern was to discover within experience some reality to which all people should be religiously committed. This reality should be concretely actual, causally efficacious, creative, and religiously absolute. In a confused and highly ambiguous world Wieman searched for an unambiguous process that is worthy of our worship and, when given the primacy of devotion, can lead to our salvation. Wieman's inquiry found its answer in the creative event or the process of creative transformation (which is alternatively called "creative interchange"). This process merits the appellation "God."

In the long odyssey involved in coming to this conclusion Wieman made two fundamental decisions. In his understanding of the Christian tradition, God is interpreted as being the unity of power and goodness, where power is defined as omnipotence and goodness is understood as consummate love. Wieman agreed with those critics of the tradition who believe this union entails the judgment that God is responsible for evil as well as being the source of good. This ambiguous God is not worthy of our worship. In order to discover a God who is free of this ambiguity, Wieman believed that one must choose between a God of goodness and a God of power. Wieman chose a God of goodness. The issue of whether this God can prevail against the powerful and demonic forces of evil is, of course, an important but not a decisive consideration.

His second decision is closely related to the first. Since there is a great diversity of kinds of processes or forces in the world, God is to be identified with that process that is truly creative of all human good (and possibly the source of the good at all levels of existence, although Wieman did not complete this metaphysical aspect of his theology). In Wieman's thought events are distinguishable basically in terms of their constituent structures. Thus the creative event has its own distinctive structure differentiating it from all other events.

In summary, Wieman's God is a God who acts in a causally efficacious manner. (Wieman's religious heritage was Calvinistic.) However, since all events are causally efficacious in one way or another, God's efficacy is distinguishable in being creatively transformative. Thus God is identified with an aspect of the world. He is one kind of process among many kinds, limited in effectiveness, but unambiguous in character and religiously trustworthy.

My contention is that Wieman's God, as defined and described, is not concretely actual. Both as a concrete process and as a process with a distinguishable and unambiguous structure, Wieman's God does not concretely exist. It is rather a high abstraction from the world of events. Wieman has described something that actually occurs, namely, the fact of transformation. He has also identified some of the phases and dimensions of this transformation. But the actuality of the process of transformation does not conform to Wieman's description of it.

The first phase of abstraction occurs with Wieman's decisions to opt for a God of goodness in contrast to a God of power and to identify this goodness with one kind of process. These decisions are translatable into a choice between kinds of causal efficacy. Wieman's God apparently does not create the world. At least He does not sustain the world as created. He is engaged solely in transforming the world as it is into something better. His activity is a particular form of creativity. These other nontransformative and inertial processes are responsible for the general creation and sustained existence of the world of concrete events.

If this is the case, then the processes of creative transformation are highly dependent upon these other forces. Without the latter, the former could not exist, although the reverse is not true. Furthermore, given the interconnectedness of events, transformative and nontransformative processes interpenetrate and participate in each other. They constitute and shape each other. The unambiguous character of Wieman's creative event is derived by abstractive separation from the convoluted web of events that in its totality may exemplify a spectrum of kinds and levels of ambiguous dynamics and structures.

Yet even this account does not get to the heart of the matter. The deeper fact is that the several phases of the experience of transformation do not in themselves constitute a concrete process or a set of processes with a distinguishable structure. The elements of a transformative experience emerge as factors within the almost infinite number of all kinds of interconnected events, of all sizes and degrees of complexity, that constitute the complex and concrete life of an enduring individual existing over an extended span of time. The variety and levels of processes, experiences, and relationships involved make demarcation literally impossible. We may isolate certain moments and results of this total phenomenon of transformation, and in our mind's eye we may connect these moments as though they constitute an actual concrete process. But this is abstraction indeed. Concretely, there is no actual and specifiable process of creative transformation. There is no creative event as such. There is, rather, a total, complex, individual life that, among other things, occasionally exemplifies transformative growth. With the recognition of degrees of relevance, it can be said that a whole complex chunk of the web of life is the source of creative transformation within the life of an individual. Wieman's God constitutes an instance of misplaced concreteness.

The criticisms of Wieman's position can also be applied to some forms of liberal theology that identified God with the "personality-producing forces of the universe" or with "a power that makes for righteousness." In all such cases the effort to live by abstracting God or the good from the concrete, living, and ambiguous realities of existence results in a loss of the sense of available resources for achieving the better.

From his study of the history of theology Whitehead concluded that the church "gave unto God the attributes which belonged exclusively to Caesar."[22] Whitehead, like Wieman, wanted to disassociate God from evil. He wanted to absolve God from any responsibility for the destructive and inertial forces at work in the world. Whitehead opted for an unambiguous deity, a God who is single-minded, unsullied, and clean.

To work out the metaphysics of this decision, Whitehead first made an ontological separation between God and creativity. God is not the creator of the world. As the principle of order God is a necessary factor in the creation of the world because without a primordial order there would be no world. But the efficacious creation of the world of actuality is not part of God's action or responsibility.

Second, God's work *in* the world is basically that of being a persuasive lure toward the achievement of qualitatively richer and more intense forms of experience. As a principle of order God operates primarily with forms. His work is mainly conceptual in nature. He arranges the order of the relevance of possibilities with respect to any occasion of experience. His conceptual functioning is to be contrasted with the physically efficacious and coercive ways of the world. To experience God is to experience a universal mind and its conceptual valuations.

To be sure, like all actual entities God has a physical as well as a conceptual side. As physical (or "consequent") God acts to preserve the values that have been realized in the actual world. This is accomplished through the agency of his physical feelings. He evaluates what He receives from the world in terms of His conceptual vision. He saves what can be saved.

But even with respect to His physical or concrete actuality we don't experience God in terms of His physical feelings. If we were to do so we would experience God as causally efficacious or as coercive. God would then be involved in evil. So we experience Him through His conceptual feelings. We experience Him as final cause, as aim, as conceptual appetition, as persuasive beckoning.

Whitehead's God receives from the world. He saves or preserves what he receives; but except for His function as a principle of order or as a conceptual lure, Whitehead's God is not involved *in* the world. Basically we know Him as a conceptual reality, as an abstract vision, as an appetition toward conceptual novelty, as an aesthetic form of persuasiveness that is pitted against the coercive and inertial powers of the world. We know Him as a conceptual urge to live well and to live better. His character is unambiguous because His reality as experienced is that of a primordial abstraction that is unaffected by the concrete world. This is the inevitable price to be paid if one's quest is for the unambiguous.

---

[22]Whitehead, *Process and Reality*, 342.

The Creative Advance

In terms of the essential understanding of the world as expressed in this essay, the creative advance of the web of life is not to be understood as an adventure toward perfection. Given the nature of the world as we experience it, the adventure toward perfection is a movement toward the vacuity of abstraction. The passion for perfection is a protest against the unmanageable vitalities of concrete life. It is a yearning for the bloodless existence of clean-cut, orderly abstractions. It is, in short, a yearning for death.

The creative advance is to be seen as a movement toward greater stature in which the zest for novel ideas of larger generality plays its needed role. This advance involves the transformation of incompatibilities and contradictions into compatible contrasts within the unity of the web and within the lives of its members.

This movement toward greater stature does not involve either the gradual or the immediate elimination of ambiguity. On the contrary, the dialectic of relationships, the dynamics of the process of becoming, and the quality of insatiable zest within the freedom of spirit move in a different direction. Even with the realization of greater stature, it would still be the case that this larger achievement will be accompanied by the possibility of greater inertial resistance of further advances. The notion of ambiguity becomes a metaphysical principle.

This view of the possible future entertains the notion that order at all levels is an emergent, that there may be no fixed and primordial order or structure, and that this may be the case whether the most general structure is viewed as ambiguous or unambiguous. This view is entertained even when the structure is defined in terms of love. This entails the suggestion that all exemplifications (as well as all understandings) of love are relativized. (The fact that most process-relational thinkers, especially theologians, hold that God has an eternal, unchanging character suggests that—in this respect at least—process-relational thought is a variation of classical thought.)

Whitehead's speculative suggestion expresses something of the spirit of this segment of the essay: "The most general formulation of the religious problem is the question whether the process of the temporal world passes into the formation of other actualities, bound together in an order in which novelty does not mean loss."[23]

The conception of the stature of God that is presupposed in this essay may be indicated by the speculative suggestion that the world is an interconnected web endeavoring to become a vast socialized unit of experience with its own processive subjectivity.

---

[23]Ibid., 340.

RESPONSE TO LOOMER

John B. Cobb, Jr. / *Claremont Graduate School*

Thirty years ago I wrote a master's thesis under Bernard Loomer's supervision. My thesis asserted Wieman's God was abstract. At the time I thought I was arguing against Loomer's position as well. Whether or not that was true then, I take some satisfaction in finding that this same thesis is a major focus of the essay we are discussing.

Nevertheless, I am not in agreement with the more basic thesis of this essay. The issue is whether, on the one hand, God is to be identified with the world or whether, on the other hand, we identify God with some aspect, or cause of some aspect, of what goes on in the world. For Loomer the question is whether God can be distinguished in any way from the totality of the world. His answer is negative. Mine is affirmative.

The issue here, I judge, is religious or existential before it is philosophical. I can accept Loomer's explanation of the meaning of the term *God,* at least in general. It is, he writes, "a symbol of ultimate values and meanings in all of their dimensions. It connotes an absolute claim on our loyalty. It bespeaks a primacy of trust, and a priority within the ordering of our commitments" (42).[1] The difference between our theories is that the world as it is in its totality does not make an absolute claim on my loyalty or establish the needed priority in the ordering of my commitments. Hence I find it incongruous to call the world God. Indeed, I find it difficult to take Loomer quite at his word when he professes the opposite position, and I seek in his essay clues as to how the differentiations, so clearly needed to order commitments, are made by him.

We have not far to go for an answer. The aim for Loomer is qualitative richness. We are to be attached to life, which means that we are to be committed to the specific processes of life. Life-determining processes should be the focus of philosophical and theological concern. Further, the directive by which we should live is found within those processes involved in sustained, mutually internal relations.

Passages such as these reassure me that, despite our differences of language and conceptions of God, our commitments are not dissimilar. What I am trying to understand is why, if Loomer's commitments are shaped in terms of specific features of the totality, the polemic against relating God particularly to these features is so sustained.

---

[1] References in parentheses are to the pages of Bernard Loomer's "The Size of God" as it appears in this publication.

Although it is clear that when Loomer says "God" he does not really mean God as the totality of all the things that collectively make up the world viewed simply, neutrally, and openly, it is not as clear that any adequate explanation is given connecting the explicit statements of God as the totality of the world with the focused commitment to life-enhancing processes and the growth of qualitative richness. Perhaps this stems from a judgment that this is what the totality is in fact accomplishing. Such an optimistic judgment about the world would indeed explain why it can appropriately be called God. The final sentence of his paper goes still further to explain why Loomer sees the world as a totality as God. "The conception of the stature of God that is presupposed in this essay may be indicated by the speculative suggestion that the world is an interconnected web endeavoring to become a vast socialized unit of experience with its own processive subjectivity".

These hints do indeed help me to understand the use of the word God to refer to the world; but they do not satisfy me. I do not want to nit-pick, but the suggestion that the world is *endeavoring* to become something, when the world now lacks unity or subjectivity, seems to reflect the fallacy of misplaced concreteness with which Loomer likes to charge advocates of other positions.

But if the world does not have this character of aiming at increasing qualitative richness through heightened interconnectedness of all its parts, and if the world is equally represented in inertial and entropic forces, as Loomer seems elsewhere to recognize, then how does calling the world God help to direct our energies toward the enhancement of life and the increase of size? It seems that when Loomer gives reasons—excellent ones—for us to direct ourselves to these ends, what he says about God in general plays no role.

The only argument I can find in his paper that really supports identifying God with the totality of the world is the argument that God must be concrete, and that every way of thinking of God other than as the totality ends up in abstractions. Yet examination of this argument weakens it. First, the words concrete and abstract are ambiguous not only in general but also in their use in this paper. Insofar as Loomer gives clear definitions he follows Whitehead, for whom only the individual, actual entity is fully concrete. Of course, societies or nexuses of actual entities also have a great deal of concreteness, but this is only the concreteness of their individual members. The closest thing in Whitehead to the totality when (as with Loomer) Whitehead's God is left out of the picture is the actual world of a particular occasion. Let us suppose that is what Loomer means by *God*. Then, strictly speaking, every occasion has a different God. Of course there are many similarities and an extensive overlap among all these Gods, and we could use the term *God* to identify these, but that would involve a major step in abstraction. God as conceived by Loomer is less concrete than God as conceived by Whitehead *if* we take Loomer's own clearest definition of concreteness, derived from Whitehead, as our criterion.

Clearly something is awry here. I think the truth is that, for Loomer, in sharp distinction from Whitehead, the concrete means physical feelings and the abstract means conceptual feelings. The argument against Whitehead is that, for him, God is felt conceptually rather than physically. Although the account of Whitehead does not seem quite accurate, I will let that pass. For at this point Loomer has something to say that persons such as myself must hear. If we think of God as the source of our conceptual feelings, at least of those not conformal to the world, and if the term *God* has the power to direct our attention and our energies, we may miss the great importance of our physical immersion in the matrix of physical things. We might slip into thinking of our physical feelings as inferior or unimportant, whereas in fact the primary role of the novel conceptual feelings is to enhance our physical enjoyment of the world and our contribution to the enjoyment of others.

I do not believe that, in order to avoid this danger, we need to identify God with the world or to assert that all of our conceptual experience is in fact derived from our physical feelings of the world. I am convinced that on these points Whitehead is wiser than Loomer, yet I am grateful that Loomer will not let us forget the richness of our physical inheritance, our indebtedness to the world as it is in its totality, and the inescapable ambiguity of all our attainments. The one-sided emphasis on creative novelty and transformation, on imagination and prophesy, on purpose and goals, needs to be checked by a deep appreciation of the interconnected matrix of worldly relations and the ways in which an interest in ideas can detract from the enhancement and enrichment of this matrix. No one can warn us of these dangers more forcefully and authentically than Bernard Loomer.

In conclusion, I would like to set this discussion in the context of world religions. Loomer's most explicit statements seem to place him close to the Taoist vision of the processive world as being what is divine; but the existential and religious meaning that Loomer draws from this reflects a quite different religious tradition, that of the West. For, though Loomer shares the Taoist polemic against the dualism of good and evil, he wants human energies actively directed to the promotion of certain types of worldly conditions rather than others—size, for example. The preference for this comes, in the Western tradition, from belief in a God who has a directive agency in history, preferring some outcomes to others.

Loomer feels that the focus on this God as distinct from the world leads us to lose the true grounding of our being and to focus on a limited aspect of our totality. I have been trying to learn a similar lesson from my reflection on Buddhism. I want to propose a position that may be more acceptable to Loomer than is Whitehead's, one that I have come to in my efforts to understand Buddhism.

There is a difference between what Whitehead calls creativity and what he calls the world. Loomer seems to subsume creativity within the totality of the world. I will not try to sort this out; however, I have become aware, as Loomer is, that Whitehead's sharp juxtaposition of God and creativity violates some very deep habits of mind that probably should be more respected. When people think of God, the kind of ultimacy Whitehead associates with creativity is often part of what they mean. Yet Whitehead is correct that when we attend to creativity as such and by itself, all possibility of establishing priorities of commitments is undercut. At one point Whitehead speaks of creativity's acquiring a primordial character, namely, what he calls the Primordial Nature of God. I think that most of what Loomer wants to say can be said in Whiteheadian terms if we identify God with creativity as primordially characterized. It is that primordial characterization that establishes the direction toward size and qualitative richness, which are as important to Loomer as they are to Whitehead and to myself. In addition, some of his talk of the world seems to include not only the totality of past actual occasions but also that principle by virtue of which they work toward size and qualitative richness in the present. If Loomer would re-define his totality to include not only what Whitehead calls the world but also what Whitehead calls the Primordial Nature of God, the gap between us would be greatly reduced.

THE AMBIGUITY OF AMBIGUITY: A RESPONSE TO LOOMER'S "SIZE OF GOD"

Delwin Brown / *Iliff School of Theology*

The structure of Loomer's argument, I believe, is as follows: (1) The concrete is more valuable than the abstract; (2) Ambiguity is essential to the concrete; (3) God is the greatest conceivable being; (4) Therefore, God is concrete and ambiguity is essential to God (44).[1]

The other and impassioned side of this argument is Loomer's warning that the denial of ambiguity in God leads to the diminution of the worth of the concrete world and our lives therein. This is the case because God is, or represents, that which is ultimately valuable (42). If God, so conceived, is in any respect unlike the concrete world in its essential features, then the world is by implication diminished in value, for the world would then differ essentially (and not merely by degree) from that which is of ultimate worth.

This argument parallels a common neoclassical theme. Contingency, change, vulnerability, and so forth, are essential features of the world. If God is the greatest conceivable being and if God is not characterized by these traits, then the world that is so characterized is somehow the antithesis of the God of value. I understand Loomer simply to be adding "ambiguity" to the list of the things the world is essentially. Just as God is, in certain respects at least, contingent, changing, and possible, so too, in Loomer's view, is God characterized by ambiguity.

Of all the claims in Loomer's essay, his basic point is not about God's ambiguity; rather, it is Loomer's insistence upon the worth of the concrete. Loomer writes, "The aim . . . is not to seek . . . ambiguity for its own sake" (43). "The elemental reason for an empirical emphasis in theology and philosophy," he tells us, is that such an emphasis promotes an attachment to the concrete processes of life (29). This commitment to the concrete is the basis of Loomer's endeavor.

I do not wish to challenge this commitment to the unqualified worth of the concrete world, nor do I wish to say anything about God that undermines this commitment, but I do have some trouble with Loomer's discussion of ambiguity. I am not convinced that his account of God's ambiguity is fully adequate.

---

[1]References in parentheses are to the pages of Bernard Loomer's "The Size of God" as it appears in this publication.

The term *ambiguity,* in Loomer's essay, refers to modes of relatedness in an occasion of experience (45), in enduring individuals (45), and in the general processes of creation (45) and our corporate lives (46-48). Surveying Loomer's statements about ambiguity suggests another classification that may be equally useful in our analysis.

Some of Loomer's statements refer to ambiguity within the sources or condition of becoming: "The unity of individuality includes an incompatibility between internalized causal influences" (45). "An individual cannot fully determine the quality of life by himself. The confusions and brokenness of his society are shaping forces within him" (45). Here the reference is to the confusion of relative goods, and the confusion of goods and evils in the objective condition of becoming, a corruption that inevitably and necessarily shapes, and indeed infects, the developing individual and society. This is what might be called an "ambiguity of condition," which pertains to all the relationships mentioned above.

Some of Loomer's statements point out the ambiguity inherent in the structure or character of becoming, considered in isolation from its objective source or condition. "Virtues and vices are inseparable with respect to origin. The good and evil of a person derive from the same origin" (47). "The passion that compels us to search for truth leads [as well] to our neuroses" (46). "The strength that is poured into the formation of our virtues is the same strength that overplays itself [into pride]" (46). "Every creative advance may give rise to its contrary" (46). Here the focus is upon the mechanism of the process of becoming. Whatever the objectively given possibilities of goods and evils, the structures of selfhood and civilization that may actualize the goods are the very same structures that may actualize the destructive potential. This could be called an "ambiguity of character."

Twice, at least, Loomer suggests a third level of ambiguity. A single decision, he says in both instances, need not be single-minded, suggesting what might be called an ambiguity of intention (45 and 46). It is not surprising that this consideration should arise, for one of the basic claims of a process-relational analysis is that each occasion of experience in the creative process is purposive or intentional. A full analysis of an occasion's becoming requires an account of its past (its "condition"), its own internal process (its "character"), and the subjective aim by which that process is organized (its "intention"). Loomer's point seems to be that this single aim "may" (his word) somehow be at odds with itself and embody contrasting impulses. While we might quarrel about how to analyze this phenomenon, I assume we would not wish to deny that it occurs. Single decisions do not need to be single-minded, hence the "ambiguity of intention."

Now the question is how, if at all, do these three types of ambiguity apply to God?

No one even remotely connected with the neoclassical position would deny that God is characterized by ambiguity of condition. Like all other entities, God cannot fully or unilaterally determine the quality of life—divine, human, or natural. The confusions and brokenness of the world are, to an unsurpassable degree, shaping forces within the life of God. There is for God, no less than for us, an incompatibility between internalized causal forces. Thus, God's "condition," like ours, is ambiguous.

Is God characterized by ambiguity of "character"? That is, can the structure of divine becoming give rise, at least in principle, to vice as well as virtue, evil as well as good? The answer of Whiteheadians will differ here depending on whether they are, in a sense, "Thomists" or "Scotists." The Hartshornians or "Thomists," for whom God's goodness is metaphysically necessary, will deny that "ambiguity of character" (as the term is here being used) applies to God—except in the very weak sense of saying that if the divine process could give rise to imperfections, the imperfections would have their origin in the same structures that give rise to the divine perfections. But Loomer emphatically rejects the metaphysical necessities of Hartshornians. Hence the Hartshornian line of argument will not prove to Loomer that God is or even could be unambiguous in this sense. The "Scotists" among Whiteheadians, holding that God's virtue is rooted in divine will or freedom and is therefore not a matter of metaphysical necessity, will side with Loomer here, at least in part. For them, God's character, or the structure of God's becoming, could give rise to vice as well as virtue, but in fact it does not. Hence, for them, God's character is in principle ambiguous, though not in fact.

It is with respect to "ambiguity of intention" that Whiteheadians will question Loomer's program and will, it seems to me, remain puzzled about the basis for that program, even from Loomer's standpoint. The reasons, I think, are as follows:

(1) While there are some respects in which a unitary decision may, and even must, be "divided against itself," there are other senses in which, in order to be a decision at all, it must be singular and unitary. That a decision must embody the need for further resolutions in succeeding moments, and might embody presently warring tensions, does not obviate the singularity of purpose that encompasses the present and potential multiplicity. To be concretely actual at all means, necessarily, to be in this sense singular and thus, in this sense, unambiguously singular. In this respect, God, like all actual entities, is necessarily unambiguous.

(2) There is another respect, however—already alluded to—in which our decisions do in fact display ambiguity of intention. We will someone's good, but then again we don't. We love, but with elements of self-seeking and hatred included in our love. There is duplicity in our singular purposings, intentional ambivalence in our singular intentions. This kind of ambiguity, I assume, is (to use Niebuhr's phrase) "inevitable but not necessary." Yet precisely because it is not necessary for us who are concrete actualities, it is not necessary for a concrete God. Thus there is no impossibility in affirming that God's intention, unlike ours, is in this sense unambiguous. If we may love unambiguously, we can say that God does love unambiguously, and we can say this without contradiction.

More important, we can say that God's intentions are pure without demeaning the concrete world. For it is precisely a capacity of concreteness as such that God's unambiguous intentions embody. If this capacity, where unrealized, is an abstraction, it is an abstraction within concreteness, not beyond it, because the realization of this potentiality—purity of purpose—in the life of one concrete being is the manifestation of the vital potentiality of all concreteness.

So far as I can tell, Loomer's affirmation of the worth of concreteness does not require a rejection of God's unambiguous goodness of intention. But perhaps Loomer is closer to the truth than we had supposed! Being neither simply one nor the other, God is ambiguous in some respects and unambiguous in others, and ambiguous ambiguity is more ambiguous than unambiguous ambiguity.

RESHAPING THE TASK OF THEOLOGY

Larry E. Axel / Purdue University

The longer I ponder the claims of Loomer's essay, "The Size of God," the more convinced I am of its profound importance; and this is not because of its exposition of the process-relational, philosophic mode, or because of its capable analysis of empirical method. Rather, the essay raises more fundamental questions concerning the nature of the theological task itself. What is the proper task of theology?

Too often in the past, theology has been seen as a quest for the unambiguous. In its search for God, insofar as God is seen as transcending all ambiguity, it has sought to resolve the ambiguities. Theology has striven to move from the concrete to the abstract, and it has identified that movement as one from less to more, but the reverse is actually the case. The flight from the concrete, the search for a transcendent that renders clear and resolves, that is unambiguous and unchanging, is actually a flight from life. Various rationalistic theodicies (seeking to explain clearly the problem of evil) are perhaps only the extreme example of this more general phenomenon. But, Loomer argues, these procedures are not truly empirical; and to the extent that they deny the concrete nature of God, they deny God's stature.

I was struck by such a denial of the concrete at a recent funeral service. Following the service Roy (my student) and I wandered slowly, and apparently aimlessly, side by side through the cemetery. The minister, in his sermon earlier inside the church, had intended to comfort, explaining Mrs. Stevens's death, portraying and clarifying the ways and purposes of God. As we walked, Roy searched for words in the midst of his grief, and said of the service: "Well, I guess maybe that helps me to understand this a little bit, to see why stuff like this happens." But I responded: "Roy, I think our purpose here is not to *understand.* We are not here to explain away, or to bring clarity to our confusion and bewilderment. What we must try to achieve is full presence with this, to let this grief flow through us, to immerse ourselves in the power and intensity and ache struggling to penetrate us, to try to practice presence, presence with her suffering and our sense of loss. What we have here is intensity of experience. Can we open ourselves to it? Can we receive it into ourselves, with its attendant pain and fullness, without needing to understand or explain?" We then fell silent, and as we walked, beside each other, immersed totally in the concrete immediacies of the event, the depth of the occasion somehow came to the fore, cradling us and even speaking through the ambiguities and confusions of this moment of intense life and death, experienced fully and painfully. Perhaps Bernard Loomer would say that we were being brought into the presence of the size of God.

If one wishes to endorse a thoroughgoing naturalism and a radical empiricism, then one must conclude that if "God" is to be known at all, God must be known in the only realm accessible to us. God will be identified either with a part or parts of the concrete actual world or with the totality of that world. Loomer maintains that to avoid a theology of abstractionism God must be seen as concretely actual, and furthermore, he claims that God therefore (as concretely actual) is ambiguous. The concretely real is always ambiguous; and the unambiguous has the status of an abstraction. Consequently, for Loomer, "an ambiguous God is of greater stature than an unambiguous deity" (43).[1] It must be immediately pointed out that the issue here is not the search for, or celebration of, ambiguity for its own sake. The key distinction is the relative richness and intensity of the concretely actual, versus that of the highly abstract. In Loomer's own words, "An ambiguous God is not of greater stature simply because He is ambiguous. His greater size derives from the concreteness of His actuality in contrast to the reality of a nonliving, undynamic, and inactive abstraction. The concretely actual is ambiguous; only the highly abstract can be unambiguous. Thus, the conclusion, and the thesis that an ambiguous God is of greater stature than an unambiguous deity" (43).[2]

In opposition to this recognition, Loomer notes that "Christian doctrines of God and Christology have been shaped by their passion for perfection or the unambiguous" (21). This is ironic, to be sure, given the roots and controlling imagery of Christian theology. To pursue this kind of abstractionism and to pay homage to perfection and the unambiguous, Christian theology has had (implicitly) to oppose the Hebrew world views that gave birth to Christianity and also has had to ignore the most fundamental implications of the Doctrine of the Incarnation. Obviously the God of Abraham, Isaac, and Jacob is not an abstraction or a general principle of order, and it would be difficult for the concreteness and ambiguity of God to be denied by anyone wishing to take the Doctrine of the Incarnation with full seriousness. Some theologies have paid a heavy price for this pursuit of perfection, for the attempts to resolve ambiguity. "Given the nature of the world as we experience it," Loomer writes, "the adventure toward perfection is a movement toward the vacuity of abstractions. The passion for perfection is a protest against the unmanageable vitalities of concrete life. It is a yearning for the bloodless existence of clean-cut, orderly abstractions. It is, in short, a yearning for death" (51). We realize, then, that theological method that seeks primarily to resolve ambiguities—given the nature of existence and the lived experience—does so at the price of eliminating concrete actuality. What does Loomer now teach us about the task of theology? There are several implications.

As we move away from a period in which people's "salvation" was said to "derive from a transcendent God to an outlook that suggests that the graces for the living of a creative life emerge within the depths and immediacies of concrete experience" (21), theology must help clarify and address the nature and resourcefulness of these depths and immediacies. Because these important resources are concretely actual, not transcendent, theology ought to assist in the immersion in life, in the intensification of experience. As such, we need to be reminded of our status as evolved earth-

---

[1]References in parentheses are to the pages of Bernard Loomer's "The Size of God" as it appears in this publication.

[2]Regarding the preservation of the original, gender-specific language, please see the note on p. 21 above.

creatures, of our affinities and interconnectednesses with the rest of nature, with the matter-energy matrix that has given us birth and of which, in some form, we shall always be a part. Aware of our immersion in this matrix, and aware of our stature as an integral part of this matrix, we see that we do not stand apart, as if observing from above. A stance of religious creaturalism, of receptivity, awe, wonder, and nature-interconnectedness is appropriate. We must deconstruct any of our theologies that claim to name ultimacies exactly, that seek a "systematic" rendering of God, that honor abstraction at the price of intensity and creatural fullness. We must seek to experience life more fully and to put theology in that service. To live a "full life" is to immerse oneself most openly and most deeply in the present at hand, attended by the living past in each moment and accompanied by the meanings portended for the future. Too often, older theologies have suggested that fullness of life has meant absence of sorrow. Concrete experience, actuality, is always clothed in ambiguity. "Grace" will come not because of any precision or because of our mapping of a transcendent power. Graces will be found in the mutually supportive relationality of the maze in which we live—fraught with ambiguity and confusion and unexpected twists and turns. As earth-creatures we do not live in straight lines; we truly do exist in a web, a network, a maze. Interconnectedness is the preeminent fact of the universe. When the relationality is mutually supportive, and not distorted, we truly can speak of "mazing grace."[3]

We suggest that one implication, then, is that there is no legitimacy to a discipline of "systematic theology"—indeed, the phrase is even to be regarded as oxymoronic. Just as most modern eschatologies have come to maintain that there is no detachable soul, so also might modern theology conclude that there is no detachable God. Theology can be systematic only if it is transcendent. If it is truly naturalistic and incarnational, then it does not have that option. Theology immersed in the concrete, and natural theology's God immersed in (or seen as?) the concrete, are, of necessity, irrevocably ambiguous.

If one adopts the general approach of "The Size of God," one does not engage in offering theodicies either at funeral services or in theology textbooks. Theodicy simply cannot—ought not—be done in the traditional manner. Yet one related issue of great import remains for our consideration here.

If Loomer identifies God with the totality of the world, conceived as concretely actual, can he avoid (ought he avoid?) an identification of God (in part) with the evil aspects of the world? As readers of his essay know, Loomer deals with this question at some length and he criticizes earlier thinkers for maintaining a bifurcation between good and evil, or God and evil. Loomer's treatment may seem puzzling to some, but it does raise provocative issues that we can only touch on here.

We can begin by noting our agreement with various attempts in the history of philosophy and theology to avoid dualism. Whitehead sought to free philosophy from various important bifurcations that had hindered its progress. Today, feminist theologians are offering the most important critiques of dualisms that have served the on-

---

[3]Compare Mark C. Taylor, *Erring: A Postmodern A/theology* (Chicago: University of Chicago Press, 1984) 168-69.

tological and social marginalization of women and that have prevented theologies from achieving wholeness and integrity. According to these dualisms (spirit and body, intellect and passion, and so forth) there are dichotomies characterized by an overside and an underside, with women always being identified with the negative pole.

So it is with the problem of evil. It has usually been suggested that there are two realities, two characters descriptive of specific aspects of the universe—good and evil. Evil is given even an ontological status. Yet we might find our way clear of Loomer's problem if we were to deny that there are any aspects of the world that are, isolatable in themselves, good or evil. In short, good and evil are not detachable parts of the universe. We ought not base our use of these terms on some split in the nature of things. In the web of life, in the world of interconnectedness, there is mutually supportive relationality. There is also what might be termed "distorted relationality," nonmutuality or disabling disintegration. This is reminiscent of Loomer's suggestion on various occasions that we should commit ourselves not to each other, but to our relatedness. We may wish to speak of evil as "distorted relationality" in a theology in which mutually supportive, internally experienced, relatedness is celebrated.

While my analysis here has been abbreviated and far from adequate, I remain convinced of the great importance of Loomer's essay, "The Size of God." Loomer's "Size" should provoke stimulating discussion for years to come. The task of theology is to speak to people's actualities, to their joys, pains, confusions, and relatednesses—even to evoke those actualities. Indeed, the task of theology is even greater: To empower the practice of authentic presence, a presence that renders internal and pervasive the fullness of life.

LOOMER ON DEITY:
A LONG NIGHT'S JOURNEY INTO DAY

Bernard J. Lee / St. Mary's University, San Antonio

A good case can be made for empirical[1] process theology as the burliest contender for being truly indigenous American theology (bur-ly adj. [ME] 1. strong and heavily built, husky; 2. heartily direct and frank). University of Chicago theologians did the pioneering: Henry Nelson Wieman and Bernard E. Meland. But the passionate energy and driving mind of Bernard M. Loomer are essential ingredients to empirical theology as a method and a movement. Loomer preoccupied himself with the methodological issues, and not with the metaphysical categories of Whitehead. Clearly indebted to Whitehead's metaphysics, he has consistently affirmed the ultimacy of becoming and the primacy of relationships. Yet in the latter stages of his reflection, Loomer distanced himself from Whitehead's natural theology and from the traditional Christian understanding of God.

Loomer's empirical commitment has had a constant moral-spiritual question for a companion: to what are communities and individuals really called? That ethical concern has marked the length and breadth of his career as a religious thinker. *Size,* of course, became his principal metaphor for both the reachings of the human spirit and the configuration of the kingdom.

His empirical commitment made him take seriously his own experience of the omnipresence of ambiguity and darkness in our world. For an empiricist, affirming the "omnipresence" of any feature of reality is tantamount to making a metaphysical judgment, which he did. "The Size of God" includes Loomer's ontology of ambiguity. Ambiguity is not something to be overcome. It is a consequence of the full, concrete richness of being. Ambiguity is normative. Ambiguity and darkness are the very stuff that provide the dialectic necessary for the acquirement of size. The structure of Loomer's argument for "The Size of God" depends upon these two interactive factors—empiricism, and size as spiritual achievement in an ambiguous world.

Loomer's essay, "The Size of God", is an assault on the traditional, Western interpretation of God precisely because it is a polemic against those Western presuppositions that were the horizon for the development of Christian doctrine: perfect rational clarity is to be sought; unambiguous goodness (like God's goodness) is the goal

---

[1]Elsewhere I have called attention to the two wings of process theology, one more rational in temper, the other more empirical. The claim I am making for "the most indigenous American theology" is for the empirical wing. Cf. my "Two Process Theologies," *Theological Studies* 45 (1984): 307-19.

of human strivings for holiness; perfect being cannot change and is not really related to the world; there are two distinct orders of being, natural and supernatural; we are autonomous individuals for whom relationship is a philosophical accident. Loomer is certainly not the first person who challenged these notions; he stands in a tradition of such challenge. Not content with seeing the problems, he formulated an alternative interpretation of deity. His alternative is likewise not brand new insofar as pantheistic identification of World and God is concerned. He is struggling for a middle ground between God the Unambiguous Person and God the Ambiguous World (at least *world* as a mere collective noun).

Personally, I believe that the details of his own speculative proposal are not, in the long run, as important as his statement of the problem—a far more difficult achievement. I see his work in ''The Size of God'' as the formulation of an agenda rather than a solution to a problem. I believe he would confirm this but he is gone now and cannot speak for himself. I think the agenda he set is crucial to the possibility of a living faith in our time. His work is an insistent rubbing of theological noses in the religious problematic of the age.

What exposure to Loomer's writing, teaching, and engaging conversation has done for me personally is send me on a theological journey that I am quite certain I would not otherwise have taken. It feels like a journey of ''hermeneutical retrieval''—recovering a biblical experience whose reality was interpreted out of existence by Hellenistic presuppositions and did not, therefore, help shape the theistic tradition that Loomer rightly criticizes. My journey presumes my agreement with Loomer's empirical commitment, with his experience of the omnipresence of ambiguity and darkness (along with clarity and light, of course), and with the general intent of his moral metaphor, size. In my reflections, I am accepting the agenda Loomer has indicated.

A key piece of the logic of Loomer's ''Size of God'' is that God must name either a part of reality or all of reality. For him the latter choice is the only way of allowing ultimate being its full, rich character as thoroughly ambiguous. My question is whether the broad experience of a long and noble religious tradition does not allow the first option—God as a being not merely identical with world, yet ''a chief exemplification'' of the world as ambiguous, shadowed, struggling, and holy precisely because of it. I also wonder whether my proposal is faithful to the agenda Loomer's essay sets for theology. I feel it is, but I will not get to hear his judgment. Between the early drafts of my paper and this essay, Bernard Loomer died. I am rather sure he would have had a lot to say about why he could not walk my road. When he would have said his ''why,'' I would have learned still more about the workings of empiricism and the centrality of moral passion.

My interaction with Bernard Loomer's ''The Size of God'' is principally from the perspective of hermeneutics: the role of metaphor in the interpretation of experience. First, I wish to reckon empirically with the metaphors of both the Hebrew Bible and the New Testament that interpret the experience of deity. I shall be concerned also with Carl Jung's interpretation of the character of human wholeness, the meaning of ambiguity and shadow, and his sense of how those experiences ought to shape our sense of deity. Fundamentally, of course, I am concerned with the metaphors Loomer uses for the same purpose. These are the principal participants in the conversation that ensues.

I Stating the Issue

Having said that God must either be a part of reality or all of reality, Loomer chooses the second: God and world are to be equated. He then examines possible senses in which "World" might be construed in the sentence "God is the World." On the one side, he rejects World as an entity that has the unity of an experiencing subject. On the other side, he rejects World as a collective noun that numerically includes all existing entities. He searches instead for a middle ground.

The World that Loomer says is God is neither a mere collective nor a living subject. However, he characterizes World-God in language that tilts metaphorically towards the notion of a personal, experiencing subject: at the "heart" of things; the world of "passion"; the world exhibits "restlessness"; there is a purposiveness expressed in "a drive to create specific kinds of relationships"; the world "struggles." In the final section of this paper, he speculates that while the World does not now have the unity of an experiencing subject, perhaps "the world is an interconnected web endeavoring to become a vast socialized unit of experience with its own processive subjectivity." In the Whiteheadian framework, much of which Loomer has accepted—"a vast socialized unit of experience with its own subjectivity"—begins to edge close to the description of person. If so, Loomer then seems to conclude that the attribution of subjectivity to World-God involves no inherent contradiction, even if it is not now the case.

I am certainly not suggesting that Loomer's World-God is a "closet person." That would exemplify on my part what Ricoeur calls "ontological naiveté."[2] I presume that Loomer's language is metaphorical. A metaphor always tells the truth on the basis of one thing being like another thing. But every "it is like that" statement has an implicit "it is not like that." Ontological naiveté ignores the "is-not." There are important "is-not's" in Loomer's metaphorical, personalistic language. I presume that Loomer's paper is a search for whatever metaphor for ultimacy is most adequate to the deliverances of lived experience.

A further indication of the metaphorical character of his exploration is the occasional use of language that in some respects is more at home in classical Christian theism—certainly not his intention. Loomer says, for example, without adding a philosophical qualification, that "we are quite literally creations of the transcendent firmament." Clearly, "transcendent" is an expression of religious sentiment and not of philosophical characteristics. Similarly, he uses a word normally associated with "infinity-type" language to say that the world is an *indefinitely* extended field of events. He does, however, add a metaphorical "it is not like" disclaimer about what he intends "indefinitely extended" to mean in his context.

Let me restate the focus of my interaction with Loomer's paper: the use of metaphor in the interpretation of experience. Increasingly for me, one of the most important testimonies Whitehead makes about the character of his work is that his technical categories "remain metaphors mutely appealing for an imaginative leap."[3]

---

[2]Paul Ricoeur, *The Rule of Metaphor* (Toronto: University of Toronto Press, 1979) 248-49.

[3]Alfred North Whitehead, *Process and Reality,* corrected edition, ed. David Griffin and Donald Sherburne (New York: Free Press, 1978) 4.

Further, I presume with Ricoeur that all thinking arises out of metaphor.[4] The nearer one gets to issues of ultimate concern or to generalization of extensive human experience, the more important it becomes to use metaphors and resist rationalizations as if they were the fuller report.

I must also say that I probably feel a little less reserved than Loomer in accessing the claims of privileged religious intuition, mystical or otherwise (Jesus' was otherwise). The difference is in degree and not kind. I seriously want to consider some biblical intuitions whose metaphors have not conditioned the Christian theological tradition in any substantial way.

I accept the agenda much as Loomer has described it. I want to inquire whether religious experience ignored or discounted by Christian theology might not facilitate a "God-as-part-of-the-world" interpretation of the nature of ultimate reality that is consistent with the program Loomer describes. To that end I will proceed to explore metaphors from both earlier (Hebrew Bible) and later (New Testament) scriptures, and then move to Jung's work.

II The Earlier Scriptures (Hebrew Bible)

Neither biblical root metaphors nor the narratives they spawn are literal descriptions of deity or attempts at metaphysics or cosmology. These images, however, do reflect a widespread experience of ultimate reality, and this experience is not to be neglected. What Whitehead said about philosophy is true about theology: we must beware of narrowness in the selection of evidence. He said we must remember that the fairies dance and Christ was nailed to the Cross.[5] I shall work my way through biblical metaphors and myths that disclose an experience of the ambiguous character of reality, God not excluded.

The scriptures are not a coherent, systematic work. They are a marvelous collection of greatly varied experiences. Therefore my conclusion about ambiguity in God is not a generalization of the whole body of biblical literature. It is, however, a large theme that runs in and out of the texts, a theme that Christian theology has not internalized but is much to the point of Loomer's concern.

The first creation account in the Book of Genesis suggests that we do not start with only God and nothing else. There is God and there is "stuff." The Hebrew word for what is already there means something akin to chaos: a waste with no definition, water and earth mingled together in primeval ooze. As creator, God intervenes in the destiny of a "stuff" that already exists with the divine. God begins by dividing light from darkness, where before they were indistinguishable. Creation is the entertainment of a new relationship between them, one that marks a quantitative leap: Our world begins.

God says, "Let us make a human person." The "us" already hints at a divine complexity. When Adam and Eve are created, there is a strange incompleteness about

---

[4]Cf. Ricoeur, *The Rule of Metaphor*, esp. chs. 2, 3, and 4; also, Sally McFague, *Metaphorical Theology* (Philadelphia: Fortress Press, 1982) ch. 1.

[5]Whitehead, *Process and Reality*, 337-38.

them because they lack that divine complexity. They are created in the image of God, but only partially. They know only good, but God knows good *and* evil. In Hebrew, "knowing" does not primarily mean a cognitive grasp of something; it means rather an immediate, direct experience. The serpent is correct: If Adam and Eve are to be like God, they must "know" both good and evil.

As only good, Adam and Eve are idiosyncratic in paradise. Even the garden has evil in it—the serpent. Further, let the landscaping of the garden not go unnoticed. The tree of life and the tree of the knowledge of good and evil are juxtaposed at the very center of the garden.

Jung suggests that the male notion of goodness involves a passion for utter perfection, for unalloyed goodness, for flawless order.[6] Adam is perhaps satisfied with knowing only good, even if the price is not yet being truly made in God's image and not yet being what Jung calls an empirical human being. Jung says that the feminine approach to goodness is in terms of integration: being able to hold complexity together in a workable unity.[7] The serpent is astute in addressing his "temptation" to become more fully human (and divine) to the woman.

In his analysis of the character of human consciousness, Whitehead stresses the importance of the negative judgment.[8] We know what something is only in contrast with what it isn't. The experience of differentiating contrast is essential to consciousness. Heightened consciousness always involves heightened contrast. One cannot know good without understanding evil. Intense consciousness, therefore, is not unmitigated pleasure; often it is a burden. Life would sometimes be far simpler if we didn't know what we know. The woman would rather sustain the discomfort of ambiguity (good *and* evil) than fail against the character of anyone's or anything's full concreteness (which choosing *only* good would do). The serpent went to the right place.

Our metaphors often know more about us than we know about them. Consider that Lucifer is the name we have given our personification of evil. Lucifer is a fallen angel, but nonetheless an angel, and therefore like all angels a son of God. Yet Lucifer is the son of darkness (as Jesus is later characterized in John as the child of light). The irony is that "Luci-fer" means "Light Bearer." The naming is not untoward. Light is often symbolically connected with consciousness. Lucifer is one of the godfathers of human consciousness, therefore of the human person as a spiritual being.

Loomer rightly notes that Christian theology has developed only the themes of light and good in God. Confronted with the biblical darkness, the Christian tradition has either affirmed a divine justice whose mystery we cannot comprehend or has implied a primitive anthropomorphism at work. But the biblical experience does not go away; there is in God an incredible darkness even as there is a love and fidelity beyond all telling. Consider the rage of a creator who destroys all life, human and animal, save one family of each species. Consider a human being turned into a pillar

---

[6]C. G. Jung, *Answer to Job* (Princeton: Princeton University Press, 1973) 33.

[7]Ibid.

[8]Whitehead, *Process and Reality,* 161, 243, 273.

of salt for looking back upon a bad place. Consider the ultimate principle of life who has angels murder the first-born sons of the Egyptians. Consider that Moses must argue God out of God's rage in order to save the Israelites in the desert.

Granted the literary character of the book of Job, it has nonetheless been admitted into the canon of scripture. This is a way of saying that truth is unveiled here. God makes a bet with Satan and, as Jung points out, "The dark deeds . . . follow one another in quick succession: robbery, murder, bodily injury with premeditation, and denial of a fair trial. This is further exacerbated by the fact that Yahweh displays no compunction, remorse, or compassion, but only ruthlessness and brutality."[9] The darkest thing of all, Jung observes, is how in the first place Yahweh ever came to make a bet with Satan that involves leading Job into temptation time after time.

The ancient Hebrew experience is confronted with what seems to be the inextricable mixture of darkness and light, evil and good. There is only one reality and all of it is ambiguous, God too. This leads Deutero-Isaiah (45:6b-7) to an extraordinary conclusion: "I am the Lord, and there is no other. I form light and I create darkness. I form good and I create evil." The logic of monotheistic faith is that this one Lord must take responsibility for all that is, no matter what, for God is the One Lord of all.

These early scriptural traditions, and especially the Isaiah text, have not conditioned Christian reflection on the issues that Loomer's article names so poignantly. Let us look also at the later Scriptures of the New Testament.

III The Later Scriptures (New Testament)

The New Testament, too, is not a univocal document. It emerges out of the experience of a range of individuals and communities. None of its varied texts has been as influential upon the formation of Christian thought as the Gospel of John. The people who forged the early Christian tradition had Greek imagination, and the Johannine Logos metaphors were especially appealing to their imagination. In John's Gospel and First Letter we find an absolutely unambiguous God who is all light, nothing but light. However, that is not the whole New Testament picture. I would like to review some of the non-Johannine materials, and then return to the Johannine experience.

How could Jesus have prayed to God, "Lead us not into temptation"? We cannot, of course, probe the subjectivity of Jesus. Yet if I look for a plausible rationale for the sixth petition of the Lord's prayer, I must remember Job's treatment at the hands of God. The text does not read, "Help me to resist temptation," and should not be construed that way to save God from the darkness hinted at there. It says, "Please, God, do not lead me into temptation; rather, deliver me from evil."

Luke gives us the parable of the forgiving father (Luke 15) who does not need and will not even listen to his wayward son's confession. He immediately orders a party when the son comes home. Here we have the full-of-love, all-light side of God. In contrast, however, recall Matthew's parable of the last-minute "guests" at a wedding feast. Those the king first invited refuse to come; each offers some excuse. In

---

[9]Jung, *Answer to Job,* 14.

desperation the king has his servants go out the into the byroads and invite anyone they find there. One of these incidental guests does not come properly dressed. The king has him bound hand and foot, and thrown out into the darkness to wail and grind his teeth. A pretty irascible king by any standards! Yet "the reign of God," Jesus instructs, "may be likened to this king." (Mt. 22:2).

In Hebrew ritual the scapegoat is an atonement symbol: the sins of all the people are placed upon the goat, which is then sacrificed. Ritual sacrifice has more layers of meaning than atonement, but that is a primary meaning. The atonement metaphor is pressed into Christological service, and its use suggests that God needs the ignominious death of Jesus to be reconciled with human history. Jung writes: "One should keep before one's eyes the strange fact that the God of goodness is so unforgiving that he can only be appeased by a human sacrifice! This is an insufferable incongruity which modern man can no longer swallow, for he must be blind if he does not see the glaring light it throws on the divine character, giving lie to all talk about love and the Summum Bonum."[10]

Let us return to John. The Gospel and his First Letter are the New Testament's witness to the exclusively "light" character of God, and of Jesus as the Incarnation of God's Logos. Consider John's prologue. The Word Incarnate in Jesus is light (1:4), and the darkness of the world is not able to overcome it (1:5). We are condemned because Jesus is light come into the world, but we have loved darkness. Evil hates light. Acting in truth means coming into the light (3:19-21). Jesus is the world's light, and no one who follows Jesus will be in darkness (8:12). Because of their faith in Jesus, his followers become children of light (12:36). John's First Letter continues the theme: God is light without any admixture of darkness (1:1:5). We cannot be in darkness and have any fellowship with God (1:1:6) or with each other (1:1:7). For Jesus and his followers the darkness is over (1:2:8).

Jung suggests that John's Gospel and First Letter are the product of rational consciousness, and especially of a masculine fixation upon clarity and unambiguous good. But the shadows of the unconscious tend not to leave us alone. Dark feelings "continued to rankle beneath the surface [of John's consciousness] and in the course of time spun an elaborate web of resentments and vengeful thoughts which then burst upon consciousness in the form of a revelation [the Book of Revelation]."[11] Whether the same person wrote both the Gospel and Letter, and the Book of Revelation (as Jung thinks) is somewhat immaterial. It could be some Johannine community seeking the same corrective that Jung imputes to a person named John. In Revelation, the God of rancor, rage, and revenge reappears. "There Yahweh again delivers himself up to an unheard-of fury of destruction against the human race, of whom a mere hundred and forty-four thousand appear to survive [Rev. 7:4]."[12] For example, to the seducer of the faithful in Thyatira, God says: "I will throw her down on a bed of pain; I will throw her and her companions into intense suffering unless they all repent, and

---

[10]Ibid., 68.

[11]Ibid., 77.

[12]Ibid., 49.

I will put her children to death'' (Rev. 2:22-23). Those who worship animals or idols will drink the wine of God's wrath and will be tormented in a lake of burning sulphur and there will be no relief day or night (Rev. 14:10-11). The Book of Revelation was probably written during intense Roman persecution. Babylon is the symbol of Rome. Chapter 18 is a sustained, black tale of the woe inflicted by God upon Rome/Babylon. This John's God is not pure, unrelieved light!

The picture of an unambiguous God, untouched by any experience of the divine's own darkness, is a quantitatively minor, rather than a major, theme in the New Testament. However, that overall minor theme is a major theme in the Johannine material that has played such a huge role in funding our doctrinal development.

I recall again, as I conclude these biblical reflections, that these accounts of God are not conscious theological reflection upon the nature of deity. They are metaphorical and mythical testimony of a widespread religious intuition into the character of ultimate reality; it is irreducibly ambiguous: good *and* evil, dark *and* light. I have not dwelt at all upon the many passages that testify to the fidelity and goodness of God—that side of the story is very familiar. I have tried to recall testimony forgotten by the theological literature of Christianity. This is the labor of hermeneutical retrieval. The retrieved darkness puts the total-light metaphor under suspicion. This is the labor of a hermeneutics of suspicion.

IV   Darkness in Jungian Thought

Whitehead describes the principle of self-transcendence in nature as the urge toward major beauty. Minor beauty is a simple, lovely, and easy harmony among parts that go easily together, but growth in the quality of spirit has rather to do with the sweaty work of transforming incompatibilities into effective contrasts and holding them within the unity of experience. Loomer addresses this issue under the notion of size: what kinds of contrasts are we able to hold together in our own experience short of spiritual disintegration?[13] Because size is a root metaphor in Loomer's value theory, it cannot but be for him a key to the nature of ultimate reality. The ability to harbor deep and uneasy contrasts is central to size. Good and evil are the test cases of contrasts.

Philosophical logic distinguishes the opposition between contradictories and that between contraries. The former are absolutely incompatible: something cannot ''be'' and ''not be'' at one and the same time from the same point of view. In the Western Christian tradition, good and evil have usually been perceived this way. Contraries have opposing thrusts, but do not cancel each other out. Loomer and Jung see good and evil as contraries. It is not so much that we have separate good and evil impulses, but that good and evil are contrary characteristics that cohabitate in the same impulses. St. Paul did not have two souls; he had one soul with two laws whose contrariness he held within him all his life. This he learned not only from the Christ event,

---

[13]Bernard M. Loomer, ''S-I-Z-E Is the Measure,'' in Bernard Lee and Harry Cargas, eds., *Religious Experience and Process Theology* (New York: Paulist Press, 1976) 70.

but from his own rabbinic tradition: the Yetzer Ra (bad impulse) and Yetzer Tov (good impulse) are pervasive in historical experience.

Only at the level of abstraction from concrete reality can one separate good from evil (thus Loomer's fear of an only-light, but abstract God). Yet that is the kind of abstraction that sunders us in our concreteness. Loomer has long insisted that God loves us not in spite of our sin, but *in* our sin; for our sin is indeed us as well as our goodness, precisely because God loves us in our concreteness. It is a sundering love that loves under abstraction. Redeeming love is never a sundering experience. Redemption does not occur because we are removed from sin, but because God has enough size to hold our sin in tension with our goodness.

For Carl Jung, darkness is not something to be overcome in order to experience light. Darkness is not simply an obstacle to holiness; darkness is an irreducible presence, and its integration is precisely the condition of increased consciousness. "Nothing so promotes the growth of consciousness as the inner confrontation of opposites."[14] Jung's *conjunctio oppositorum* (the conjoining of darkness and light) is analogous to Loomer's size. Darkness is singularly destructive when we ignore it or presume that we have eliminated it. The integration of darkness is not simply a matter of saying yes to evil, but of saying yes to the whole being in whom the Yetzer Ra coexists with the Yetzer Tov and can never be excised.

With his ontology of darkness and light, Jung addresses the wholeness and holiness of God. He cites Clement of Rome's image that God rules the world with two hands: the right hand is Christ and the left hand is Satan. With the logic of an Isaiah, Jung observes that "if Christianity claims to be a monotheism, it becomes unavoidable to assume the opposites as being contained in God."[15]

Jung has said that whether or not the human race comes to full-scale nuclear war depends upon whether enough people are able to address their darkness.[16] Barbara Hannah, who had a long apprenticeship with Jung, suggests that the source of violence in the Western soul is our not having been able to come to terms with our darkness (to which the rhetoric of Reagan's description of Russia as "an empire of evil" testifies). If our image of ultimacy is that of an absolutely unambiguous source of pure light, then we are condemned to disallow our darkness and therefore deprive it of its potential gift of spiritual being. To construe meaning in that way creates a split in reality—an unambiguous God and an ambiguous history. That split in turn becomes the deep rift in human souls that Barbara Hannah describes. The rift exacerbates our propensity towards violence.

Jung (and Hannah) move into metaphysical speculation from deep immersion in experiences of the human soul: what it is like to be a human person striving for spiritual stature; what do we do with our darkness so as not to treat it as a lie but as life; and what understandings of the nature of reality are intuited from the character of that struggle. In that context, she says that "we must choose between a dualistic concep-

---

[14]C. G. Jung, *Memories, Dreams, Reflections,* recorded and ed. Aniela Jaffe (New York: Vintage, 1965) 345.

[15]Jung, *Answer to Job,* x.

[16]Barbara Hannah, *Encounters with the Soul* (Santa Barbara: Sigo, 1981) 8-9.

tion of God (God and his enemy the devil) or admit that God himself contains both sides and is thus truly whole and omnipotent. If one has experiences of how relative and totally different the opposites become when both are fully accepted, it is not difficult to imagine a God who contains both opposites.''[17] The acceptance of the darkness is not an acquiescence in evil.

What is at stake here is a fundamental presupposition about the nature of moral goodness. For the Greeks it was the complete absence of evil, the total victory; however, in an important strain of the Hebrew experience, goodness consists rather in integrity, the ability to hold all our reality together in our love. The Greek God is perfect because of the absence of evil. The Hebrew God is holy because of the integration of all impulses into a life-giving mode of being. Fidelity is a foundational characteristic of God's holiness and is related to God's size. To be faithful to a people is to refuse to forsake them in spite of their evil. They must be held in all their loveliness and all their terror in God's faithful love, by that same God who first formed light and created darkness. Hannah begs us to ''reconsider our inborn conception of God Himself in the light of Isaiah's little known description of him [Is. 45:6b-7].''[18] Loomer asks that we radically reappraise our notion of deity for similar reasons. When Jung proposes a God who embraces good and evil impulses in the essential structure of his own experience, he recognizes, of course, that he is moving in a world of images; he does not pretend to touch the essence of God.[19]

Loomer and Jung both approach the issue of ultimacy from the framework of values. For Jung it is integration or individuation. For Loomer it is size. People who experience ultimacy ransack everything at their disposal—symbols, metaphors, myths, concepts—to proclaim the experience. Loomer ransacks his world of values. From there size is cultivated as a primary metaphor for his elucidation of the experience of ultimacy.

I have tried to say in my reflections thus far that Loomer is a kindred (though not identical) spirit to the Hebrew experience of holiness and the Jungian experience of wholeness.

V   In Search of Metaphor

I accept, with Richard Rorty, the image (borrowed from Gadamer) of philosophy as conversation about ultimate issues. This conversation is thoroughly conditioned by one's times and concerns. Because of its conditioned nature, it is always partial in its report.[20] It is not ''mere'' conversation; it is precisely this kind of conversation that constitutes our culture. I would add, from Ricoeur, that this conversation originates in a primordial metaphorical grasp of experienced reality.

---

[17]Ibid., 247.

[18]Ibid., 246.

[19]Jung, *Answer to Job*, xiii.

[20]Richard Rorty, *Philosophy and the Mirror of the Mind* (Princeton: Princeton University Press, 1980) esp. chs. 7 and 8.

Theology, too, is such conditioned conversation. It is rooted in metaphor. It plays a constitutive role in the sociocultural system of a faith community. We cannot escape the conditioned character of being and knowledge. However, this relativity is not just a function of our limits; it is also where the inexhaustible richness of being shows itself. In "The Size of God" Loomer writes that "the unremovable arbitrariness of the premises of meaning that ungird our systems of explanation symbolizes the immanence of the mystery of existence that absorbs not only our questions but also our deep-rooted criteria of value and intelligibility" (25-26).[21]

Let me return to Loomer's critique of the received Western tradition: "The God of our fathers was an infinite God": unlimited, all good, and so forth; this is basically accurate. However, the "fathers" are those who formed the Western Christian tradition, and they are not the total content of the Judeo-Christian tradition. Western Christian theology ignored the biblical report of God that seems to show the struggle of God with God's own darkness, even as divine love for the world engages God in the world's struggle with its own darkness. It is Loomer's conviction, based on his interpretation of the deliverances of experience, that the world in which we live cannot support the hypothesis of unambiguous being.

In my judgment Loomer does not simply argue with the tradition. Although it is not his specific, conscious intention, he reopens the God question to some formidable resources in the broader Judeo-Christian experience. When that broader tradition is accessed, we cannot speak of the infinite God of our fathers and mothers as the whole of the Judeo-Christian tradition.

I want to return again to the other half of his argument, the framework of moral concern. How do people and systems become holy? They open themselves to size. How much life can you take in? How much world can you absorb, even when you know that taking it in means the total embrace of an irreducibly ambiguous reality? Affection for the world is a prerequisite. That is, an affection that puts the heart under the extraordinary requirement to increase its power to love. There is a style of life at stake: "The translation of this mode of thought into a style of life is premised upon what may be called an 'attachment to life' . . . a persistent and spirit-testing commitment to the processes of life, as a discerning immersion in what is most deeply present at hand and concretely at work in our midst. The cultivation of this commitment is the elemental reason for an empirical emphasis in theology and philosophy" (29). He ransacks a value system for a metaphor of ultimacy, and thereby suggests a new hermeneutical structure within which I think it is possible to reassess the full body of biblical experience. However, I do not want to underestimate the radical character of his speculative work; it is far from a mere repetition of the religious intuition of God, Adam, Eve, and the snake. Its most radical position is not so much making room for the darkness of God, it is rather in positing that the equation of God and World is the only (or best) way to do justice to the experience of ambiguity in a world that, due to ambiguity, is engaged in a life-giving struggle towards stature of spirit.

---

[21]References in parentheses are to the pages of Bernard Loomer's "The Size of God" as it appears in this publication.

I acknowledge my natural propensity to understand God as one being that inter-acts with self and all other beings in the world—the option that Loomer did not select for the reasons he has given. I know that I lean this way partly because the fuller biblical tradition out of which I come seems to make room for the darkness and strug-gle of God within the context of a being for whom metaphors of personhood are more adequate than impersonal metaphors. Since, as Loomer presumes, the world is a re-lational web in which all parts have impact upon all other parts, and vice versa, the influence of one (divine) being upon all others, and of all others upon that one does not involve inherent contradiction (so long as that being shares in the ambiguity of the world). Further, as I have already pointed out, Loomer himself uses psycholog-ical, personal metaphors for describing World-God ("struggles, has passion, has heart," and so forth). Although he does not see evidence for affirming that World-God *now* has the unity of an experiencing subject, he is also open to the speculation that the World-God is "endeavoring to become a vast socialized unit of experience with its own processive subjectivity" (51). If that were the case, this World-God for whom the metaphor of "person" might become more accurate would still not have the personhood attributed to Yahweh. Yahweh is not all the world, but rather a part (though the crucial part without which the rest could not exist). The one point I am making is that Loomer's position does not seem a priori closed to *a* God with per-sonal qualities.

One advantage of reinterpreting God through metaphors of both ambiguity *and* person is that it makes the revision easier to assimilate within the Judeo-Christian tradition. "Easier" doesn't mean it would be a pushover. However, I would cer-tainly not propose one interpretation over another because it is more palatable. An ambiguous Person-God is the report upon deity that issues from widespread religious intuition within the sacred texts of the tradition itself. My reason for choosing the metaphor of person is an empirical reason, not a rhetorical one.

There are concerns that favor Loomer's proposal. Although he finally disagrees with Wieman's natural theology because Wieman makes God into an abstraction, his concerns are deeply resonant with those of Wieman. On the basis of these concerns, Loomer's World-God has a strategic metaphorical advantage over Person-God.

In his "Intellectual Autobiography," Henry Nelson Wieman writes:

> Transformation can occur only in the form of events. The empirical method is the only possible way to distinguish events and to know what transformation results from them. Therefore, if the religious problem be as stated, theology must be empirical . . . . God is what transforms man as he cannot transform himself, to save him from self-destruc-tive propensities and lead him to the best that human life can attain . . . . Nothing can transform man unless it actually operates in human life. Therefore, in human life, in the actual process of human existence, must be found the saving and transforming power which religious inquiry seeks and which faith must apprehend.[22]

---

[22]Robert W. Bretall, ed., *The Empirical Theology of Henry Nelson Wieman* (Carbondale IL: Southern Illinois University Press, 1969) 3-4.

Wieman and Loomer (Wieman's student) are equally and profoundly attached to this life as the only place where redemption can occur. To rephrase Tillich, the relational web is the structure of grace in history. That is consonant with Jewish Scriptures and Hebrew instincts: redemption is found only and always through the processes of historical experience. Any interpretation of God that would turn our eyes or redirect our energies and commitments away from the actual processes of human existence could not, for Loomer or Wieman, tell the truth about God.

In Loomer's speculative proposal, World-God has the metaphorical advantage over the traditional, personal interpretation of God because it disallows any trust outside of the boundaries of the concretely real, empirical world of relational events. In the theological and liturgical traditions of Christianity, there has been much turning away from those processes of human existence, away from the requirements of the relational web. That long, two-world Christian tradition cannot but haunt even a radically revised understanding of a personal God. It would be difficult to keep that personal God so worldly that one never takes leave of that worldly God's world. The Jewish experience of God in the Hebrew Scriptures was one that enhanced and never demeaned history as the only theatre for the drama of the covenant. It would be a struggle, in the best of circumstances, for twentieth-century Christians to recover that Godly attachment to the processes of history that, as Loomer announces, is clearly his program: "Truth exists for the sake of value. The value that is at stake in a commitment of attachment is the value of the relational life in its deepest meaning" (30). Even so, it is clear to me that Loomer does propose World-God for a strategic reason, even if there are certain such rhetorical advantages. For him, it is the inexorable requirement of the deliverances of experience.

I want to note a remarkable resemblance between Loomer's theistic proposal and the Christological proposal of Pierre Teilhard de Chardin. "Christ" is used in several related ways by Teilhard. The one that Loomer's proposal resembles is that of a world that is quite literally moving towards a new mode of being in which the world itself gains in spiritual centeredness and becomes hyperpersonal. Teilhard suggests that the entire world is gradually becoming personalized as "a new form of biological existence,"[23] which marks an advance "in some sort of supreme consciousness."[24] In other words, the world grows into a new kind of centeredness and becomes a personal whole in a way in which it was not originally constituted. There are many important differences between Teilhard and Loomer, but the analogy between World-God's acquiring its own processive subjectivity and World-Christ's becoming hyperpersonal is indeed noteworthy.

VI Conclusion

I have agreed solidly with the empirical method as described by Loomer. I concur with his characterization of reality as ultimately becoming and primordially relational. I agree with his approach to the moral life, with his sense of the human spirit

---

[23]Pierre Teilhard de Chardin, *The Phenomenon of Man* (New York: Harper & Row, 1961) 303.

[24]Ibid., 258.

reaching for a "size," without which the world may not survive. I also experience, as he does, the omnipresence of ambiguity and darkness. Out of all of these, the God issue he raises is crucial to the continuing possibility of faith in God.

I believe Jung's judgment that history will be in increasingly serious trouble if we do not find a way to live with our darkness, a holy way to embrace it and include it in ourselves. We cannot hate or deny our darkness, our mixture of good and evil, and survive as a human race. Neither can we not hate it if its existence is not legitimated by how we experience and interpret the ultimate nature of things. If our symbolic structure does not allow us to be holy like God even as we are darkness and light together, we cannot say yes to our own lives, and the guilt-rift in the Western soul deepens. If Loomer and Jung are correct, the rift is there because we have worshiped a false God, and they—each in his own way—offer new root metaphors for the interpretation of deity.

I have already posed in question: is it not possible, within Loomer's empirical rubrics and their concomitant logic, to interpret God as "a" being rather than "all" being, and also as thoroughly "worldly" and ambiguous? There is experience in the Judeo-Christian tradition for thus conceiving of deity. My experience leads me in that direction.

Equally, I admit, there are reasons for skepticism about whether this is radical enough to shake Christian history loose from its destructive attachment to nonambiguity and its deadly fear of its own darkness before it is too late. Loomer's World-God is a far more radical proposal.

There is a materialist ethic that refuses to manifest itself in the world as anything more than a collective. And there is a transcendental ethic that refuses to take the world with ultimate seriousness. Loomer addresses the crucial issue of a religious understanding of deity that will not participate in either of these refusals.

TAKING MEASURE OF "THE SIZE OF GOD"

Nancy Frankenberry / Dartmouth College

Judging from the responses included in this volume, measure has been taken of "The Size of God" and it falls somewhat short. The theological concerns expressed by John Cobb, Delwin Brown, Bernard Lee, and Larry Axel vary, but each raises searching questions that Loomer's programmatic essay does not entirely address. My own purpose will be to try to assess and amplify these questions, bringing Loomer's perspective to bear on the critical responses to his work.

Of the issues John Cobb has identified, I think three deserve further examination: (1) Loomer's inclusive identification of God with World, (2) the confusing use of the categories *concrete* and *abstract,* and (3) the appropriateness of what Whitehead termed the Primordial Nature of God for establishing the direction toward size and qualitative richness that Loomer prizes. The resolution of each of these points seems to me to depend upon an evaluation of Loomer's understanding of the role of causal efficacy in the creative advance.

Cobb has located the first issue between himself and Loomer in the question of whether God is to be identified with the World (Loomer's thesis) or with only some aspect or cause of some aspect of what goes on in the world. Important and probably irreconcilable religious differences make this question more than purely philosophical. Religiously, Cobb stands with those who find some events far more revelatory of God's character than other events, in a way that makes an "absolute claim" on his loyalty and that establishes priority in the ordering of commitments.

Loomer's strategy, as far as I can see, is not to dispute this stance so much as to blur our conception of the character of any class of events that could be taken as making an absolute claim on our commitment. What is more, he thinks that we do not have, and cannot get, any formal criteria that will help us decide in advance how to focus commitment to life-enhancing processes and the growth of qualitative meaning rather than to their opposites. Size, as Loomer's criterion of interpretation, signifies an ex post facto measurement of value, but size as an achievement need not be an unmitigated good. One who is committed to the relational *process* that makes for size, rather than to its end product, may still come out with a pretty poor mess. Life is lived in the presence of something that is radically free and compulsive, according to Loomer, but not for that reason blind or unordered. It has its dark side and its death-dealing aspects as much as it has what Loomer calls "the quality of insatiable zest within the freedom of spirit" (51).[1]

---

[1]References in parentheses are to the pages of Loomer's "The Size of God" as it appears in this publication.

It is true that the possibly ever-enlarging size Loomer envisions for God is a function of precisely the kind of process that Wieman depicted as "creative event" and that Cobb has developed in terms of "creative transformation."[2] Although Loomer charges Wieman with abstractionism in his conception of God, he nowhere disagrees with Wieman's statement that "the goal of life is to structure the world so that qualities will be more appreciable. The qualities of the world become more appreciable as they are connected with one another by way of meaning and are so related as to vivify one another by contrast."[3] Why then does Loomer not also directly and exclusively identify the meaning of God with the value-producing events within the totality?

Part of the problem in pinning Loomer down on this question is that his prose does not easily convey his meaning. What Loomer really means by the "totality" or the "web of life" is not what is ordinarily meant by "world," either as the sum aggregate of all the things there are or as the logical structure of reality. In Loomer's view, creativity itself, as the process of the many becoming one and being increased by one, is a dynamic process that takes on different structures and is itself undergoing change. Thus, what is distinctive about Loomer's discussion is the challenge it offers to both the Wiemanian and the Hartshornian view of the character of the divine existence as an unchanging one. The dynamic view of creative synthesis implied in Loomer's understanding of size is concerned with the possibility of a self-surpassing even of the abstract structural character of the divine existence. In this he takes a cue from Whitehead, who indicated that there is no reason why extension should not exemplify an indefinite number of dimensions, in contrast to the three dimensions of space that now obtain in this cosmic epoch. If indeed other dimensions of extension were ever to emerge, the character or order of the world would be transformed in kind and not simply in degree. Do analogous possibilities apply also to the size of God? Loomer's hypothesis is that the dimensions that presently prevail and the Hartshornian analysis of the logical structure of reality need not be taken as exhaustive or definitive. If the theory of emergence applies not only to the world but also to God, then there is no fixed, unchanging essence even of God's abstract character.

The most important feature of Loomer's approach, which is obscured by his terminology, is the emphasis he places on Whitehead's notion of causal efficacy. Cobb is probably wise not to try to unpack Loomer's ambiguous use of the terms *concrete* and *abstract,* and *physical* and *conceptual,* or his warrants for subsuming within the totality of the world the Whiteheadian notion of creativity. Systematic problems of Whiteheadian interpretation are involved here, and Loomer does nothing to resolve them.

In this essay, and elsewhere, he has a tendency to conflate the Whiteheadian meanings of causal efficacy, creativity, efficient causality, physical feelings, and concreteness.[4] Taken in Loomer's idiosyncratic usage, the sharp distinction between

---

[2]Cf. Henry Nelson Wieman, *The Source of Human Good* (Carbondale IL: Southern Illinois University Press, 1946) and John Cobb, *Christ in a Pluralistic Age* (Philadelphia: Westminster Press, 1975).

[3]Wieman, *The Source of Human Good,* 304.

[4]Cf. also Loomer's conflation of these terms in the transcript of his remarks in "Meland on God," printed in the *American Journal of Theology & Philosophy* 5 (May and September 1984): 138-43. The best interpretation of his position is that Loomer views any instance of causal efficacy as inclusive of final causality, as well as efficient causality. His discussion of the Whiteheadian category of physical feelings within the context of causal efficacy is a way of trying to restore the physical, but not to the exclusion of conceptual feelings.

concreteness and abstraction can lead to a disabling antithesis between "empirical" and "rationalistic" forms of process thought, as though they are distinct alternatives rather than complementary emphases. Loomer did as much as anyone to foster this division. I do not think it will stand up. Even for radical empiricism, experience includes both concrete and abstract dimensions, which are not, strictly speaking, correlative with the belabored distinction between particulars and universals.

Therefore, dropping the language of physical and conceptual feelings, I think it is more helpful to consider the role of causal efficacy within Loomer's empiricism. This is the true locus of "concreteness" in his discussion, from which any subsequent distinction between final and efficient causality would have to be understood as analytic abstractions. Without the operation of causal efficacy as the ground of all interconnectedness, there is no emergence, no lifting of life to new levels. Emergence requires the presence of self-creativity on the part of processive-relational data. Apart from the relational data that embody causal efficacy, there is no self-creativity, no freedom, no self-transcendence, in short, no qualitative emergence.

The notion of size captures Loomer's point that the more complex the process of integration, the greater the freedom, and the greater the possibility of qualitatively higher forms of emergent actuality. If the concept of emergence can be generalized to apply to the reality of God, as Loomer hypothesizes, then two consequences are entailed for process theology. First, real possibilities are emergent. Second, the very character of God, as a structure of concrete occasions and their relations, would also be understood as potentially capable of undergoing transformation. Size, Loomer is claiming, contains its own appetition toward self-transcendence. This is his empirical equivalent to Hartshorne's conception of the necessary existence of God.

The difference may become more apparent if we realize that Loomer is pointing to a *possibility* of God's size, not to an actuality. Thus, the "optimistic judgment about the world" (which Cobb remarks on) in the statement that closes Loomer's essay should not be exaggerated. Yet how are we to interpret Loomer's claim that "the conception of the stature of God that is presupposed in this essay may be indicated by the speculative suggestion that the world is an interconnected web endeavoring to become a vast socialized unit of experience with its own processive subjectivity" (51)? How well does this fit with William Dean's view that Loomer became less "rationalistic" and more "empirical" in the last decade of his life? What could be more rationalistic, speculative, and nonempirical than the idea of the totality—unless it is the idea of the totality tending toward possibly ever-greater size?

Loomer's remarkable sentence is, I suggest, an alternative expression of his statement in 1969 that to define the concrete nature of God up to the limit of a rational-empirical approach "would imply that God's concrete unity is a growing or developing unity, an emergent. Concretely, God would be one process among several, and the idea of the universe as one organic unity might constitute an ideal to be achieved. Again, unity would not be a given, but a future emergent."[5] Loomer's position in "The Size of God" differs from this earlier statement only in terms of a less

---

[5]"Empirical Theology within Process Thought," in *The Future of Empirical Theology,* ed. Bernard E. Meland (University of Chicago Press, 1969) 168.

equivocal willingness to follow such a speculative lead. The point, in each case, is that the speculative hypothesis concerns a *future* creative synthesis that may possibly become emergent from present relational processes. But it is not a given actuality. Reality is still in the making, change changes, and the structure of change itself undergoes change. Process is not sheer ongoingness. If this is so, then the question Loomer poses is: why suppose any metaphysical limits at all to the cosmic advance, even those that seem to pertain within Whiteheadian or Hartshornian construals of metaphysical first principles?

Cobb's final suggestion is that Loomer could redefine his conception of totality to include the recognition that creativity is primordially characterized, and that this would establish the direction toward size and qualitative richness that both he and Loomer value. I fully appreciate the metaphysical coherence that this move introduces in Whitehead's system, but I doubt that it is compatible with Loomer's explicit adoption of George Herbert Mead's position—against Whitehead's—that possibilities, and not only actualities, are also emergent in time.[6] Ironically, Loomer is probably closer to Hartshorne here than anywhere else. Both Hartshorne and Loomer would streamline Whitehead's conception of the primordial nature of God, jettisoning any permanent structure of possibility as unwanted, metaphysical baggage. Real possibilities are to be understood as emergent from the settled totality of past actual occasions. For Hartshorne, however, logical possibilities are a priori, eternal, and necessary. For Loomer, concrete historical processes are all we have, as William Dean notes.

Is there, regarding these terms, a way of talking about an impulse toward size or qualitative richness within concrete historical processes? Yes, but not by employing a *principle* by virtue of which the world tends toward anything. Loomer's empiricism permits no such primordial principle except as a descriptive generalization of the way in which relations are actually coordinated in experience. Yet even if his radical empiricism does not support the full size of God as a metaphysical *given*, it does permit it as a *possible* emergent.

Delwin Brown understands Loomer simply to be adding the quality of "ambiguity" to the list of the features that essentially characterize one pole of dipolar theism. Just as Hartshorne's neoclassical theism has introduced "contingency," "change," "relativity," and so forth into the concrete actuality of God, Loomer could be interpreted as recommending the attribute of "ambiguity." But Loomer meant more than this, I believe. Ambiguity entails something more than just another variation on the neoclassical theme. It issues in a challenge to the very idea of a priori truth. It also serves to undercut neoclassical theism's axiom that the *abstract character* of God's dipolar unity is fixed and essential, not changing or evolving beyond itself.

---

[6]Loomer did not accept the view that in the Whiteheadian system God is necessary to account for an ordered hierarchy of possibilities in relationship to any concrete situation (see, for instance, his statement in "Meland on God," 141). Unfortunately, he never worked out the systematic implications of this view in a way that might have contributed to the "Whitehead without God" debate. For this discussion, see Donald Sherburne, "Whitehead without God," in *Process Philosophy and Christian Faith*, ed. Delwin Brown, Ralph E. James, Jr., and Gene Reeves (Indianapolis: Bobbs-Merrill, 1971) 305-28, and the ensuing exhanges between Sherburne and John Cobb in *Process Studies* 1 (1971) and 2 (1972).

Brown's helpful analysis of the differences among "an ambiguity of conditions" of past data, "an ambiguity of character" internal to a present process, and "an ambiguity of intention" in subjective aim furnishes a good framework for considering just how radical Loomer's theistic proposal is. Brown asks how these senses of ambiguity are to be understood as applying to God. Given the long-standing neoclassical emphasis on the "ambiguity of conditions" even within the life of God, the issue between Hartshorne and Loomer divides on the question of God's ambiguous *character* and *intention*. Brown disputes the idea that there could be any "ambiguity of intention" in God any more than in any actual entity that must embody a singular and unitary decision in order to be anything actual at all. It seems clear to me that Loomer could not deny this. But on the assumption that God's aim is for the greatest possible size (the most general dimensions of aesthetic order), Loomer would still leave open the possibility that the process of transforming incompatible relations into effective contrasts could issue in the emergence of qualitatively new dimensions even of the abstract character of what is meant by God.

The second respect in which Brown finds it possible to affirm an unambiguous intention or "goodness" in God depends upon making the neoclassical distinction between "love" as exemplified by finite, contingent creatures and as exemplified unsurpassingly by God. Within our singular purposings, definite decisions, and decided outcomes can be found all the conflicting elements that Reinhold Niebuhr acutely exposed. These may be "inevitable but not necessary." Surely Loomer, whose own debt to Niebuhr is conspicuous, would agree with this much. But he breaks with Niebuhr at a crucial point—one about which Brown has reservations. Both Niebuhr and Brown want to affirm an unambiguous love and an unambiguous intention in God. Loomer, as I read him, wants to insist not only on a factor of historical, but also of ontological, ambiguity. Those actualities that create human life also destroy. Creative and destructive processes are correlative and inseparable aspects of the sustaining environment. We may choose to say that we worship only the god who is creative of human life and transformative of evil, but nevertheless the creative processes that constitute the "web of life" also function to destroy; everything is bought with a price.

It is not Loomer's intention, any more than it is Brown's or Cobb's, to identify the object of religious commitment with a hypostasized class characteristic, creativity as such. For religious reasons, Loomer is not willing to equate the theistic object with sheer creativity, in the sense that the cosmos is conceived simply as the onrushing upswell of unforeseeable form. Like Whitehead, Loomer discerns certain ordering principles such that creativity is viewed as having aims beyond sheer fecundity. It wants certain kinds of shapes, forms, ways of togetherness at certain times; it aims at value. Therefore, Loomer has opted theistically not for a deity of sheer, directionless creativity or pure will in the Schopenhaurean sense, but a deity of order and an urge toward value. Even so, he finds no empirical basis for affirming an unambiguous intentionality to this urge. The "goodness" and the "love" that might be attributed to God as so conceived may bear little resemblance to the human meanings of these terms.

Going beyond this, Loomer's preoccupation with ambiguity extends to the more generalized dimensions of "the web of life." One way of interpreting his notion of ambiguity, shorn of any language about divine intentionality, is to compare it with David Bohm's work on an implicate order in quantum physics. According to Bohm, "if relativity theory were able to explain matter, it would say that it would be all one form—a field—all merging into one whole. Quantum mechanics would say the same thing for a different reason, because the indivisible quantum links of everything with everything imply that nothing can be separated."[7] Still, it is not yet clear, even from recent discussions, that the implicate order of Bohm's whole-and-parts model permits the kind of qualitative emergence that Loomer's model seeks.[8]

Bernard Lee has asked whether it is possible, within Loomer's empiricism, to interpret God as "a" being rather than "all being," still retaining the rest of Loomer's program. I think not. Unless one is prepared to go in the direction of Wieman, or in the direction of Hartshorne, the notion of "a" divine being, however complex such a being is within process-relational categories, is the end product of precisely those abstractive modes of thought that Loomer finds unwarranted. In neither case could the unity of God be established empirically. Loomer has shown exactly why, according to radical empiricism, the *unity* of God-World is a difficult notion to sustain.

Why would an empirical theist be bothered by the question of the unity of that which is designated "divine" in naturalistic terms? Lee is bothered, apparently, because of his interest in tilting the discussion toward the notion of god as a personal, experiencing subject. His sensitive and suggestive retrieval of scriptural metaphors and Jungian motifs may indeed accord well with Loomer's own figurative or poetic flourishes in speaking of a "passion," a "restlessness" at the "heart of things," where there is a "drive to create certain kinds of relationships" as the world "struggles" toward greater size. Despite this, I think that Loomer would reply that Lee has an uphill battle ahead of him if he proposes to reinstate personal language, even metaphorically, about God. The very meaning of the claim that God is personal has become one of the most difficult theological questions of this century. Most religious naturalists like Loomer could understand what is affirmed by Lee's speaking of "a God with qualities of person" if this is taken to refer to the *relationship* to that which is conceived as God. In fact, this seems to be the affirmation intended by a wide variety of contemporary theologians. Lee makes a splendid case for the classification of such language as metaphorical. Still, we might wonder how much of an advance this finally is on the Thomistic category of analogy. Whether the proper category is "symbolic," "metaphorical," or "analogical," the issue remains that of a chasm between the language of devotion and the language of reflection. Has twentieth-century theological reflection made good on its defense of a "personal god," or has it largely succeeded in showing the incoherence of such a notion? My judgment is that, at least in Loomer's naturalistic, theistic framework, it hardly makes sense to attribute qualities of person or of intelligence and purpose to the world-totality.

To many of us it makes even less sense to view Loomer's theistic proposal in conjunction with Teilhard de Chardin's christological proposal, a resemblance Lee notes in passing. If apt, Lee's analogy between Loomer's World-God acquiring its

---

[7]David Bohm, "The Implicate Order: A New Order for Physics," *Process Studies* 8 (1978): 90. See also his *Wholeness and the Implicate Order* (London: Routledge & Kegan Paul, 1980).

[8]See, for example, the interesting range of essays in *Physics and the Ultimate Significance of Time: Bohm, Prigogine, and Process Philosophy.* ed. David R. Griffin (Albany: State University of New York Press, 1985).

own processive subjectivity and Teilhard's World-Christ becoming hyperpersonal may be very suggestive.

What it suggests to me is the extremely tenuous basis of the whole hypothesis. To the extent that any specifically religious categories are pertinent to the soaring vision of Loomer's closing statement, they seem to be those of hope, trusting expectation, and covenantal faithfulness—in the face of no assurances. Forsaking both an older, theistic trust in the ultimate goodness of being and a newer, existentialist attitude of defiance in the face of an indifferent universe, Loomer's brand of radical empiricism, like James's, affirms the risk and adventure of an unfinished universe. Refusing either ultimate optimism or ultimate pessimism about the human condition, it is content with meliorism. The ambiguous nature of the web of historical experience gives no destiny. It permits something more—an open future, of possibly greater unity. This does not secure our projects from shipwreck nor does it promise that unity is anything other than a contingent emergent. The Christian Gospel, as Loomer used to point out, has never promised anything more.

On other counts, Lee's reflections, many of them arising out of biblical hermeneutics as well as Jungian thought, hold the promise of a very different kind of process theology. If I may extrapolate from his rich paper, I would cite the following recommendations for the development and correction of process theologies: (1) a profounder sense of ambiguity in theological language about "the whole," (2) a more dialectical incorporation of the sense of mystery as a qualification, finally, of the status assumed or claimed for the strictly metaphysical deployments of process thought, and (3) the retrieval of the Jewish roots of Christianity and greater attention to post-biblical, Jewish traditions on the part of Christian process theologians.

Larry Axel's reflections on "Reshaping the Task of Theology" deliver a sharp blow to the very idea of a systematic theology. In light of Loomer's radical critique of the tradition, Axel has posed fundamental questions concerning the nature of the theological task itself. Particularly provocative is his suggestion that, as an implication of Loomer's approach, there is no legitimacy to a discipline of "systematic theology." Axel appears to have transposed Loomer's category of ontological ambiguity and applied it even to second-order reflective discourse *about* ambiguous realities. This strikes a questionable bargain. Why should abstraction, precision, and organization (which Axel associates with "systematic") be taken as antithetical to the rational effort of attending theologically to concrete experience? If the "web of life" is indeed more than metaphor, can we afford to give up the necessity of trying to frame a "systematic" account of it? Are we not driven to systematic reflection precisely *because* of the ineradicable feature of ambiguity in concrete experience? My own suspicion is that theologians in the tradition of radical empiricism have leaned one-sidedly toward an emphasis on the second half of Whitehead's admonition to "seek clarity, and distrust it." The first injunction is to *seek* clarity, and systematic rigor would seem to be essential to that seeking.

Given Axel's conception of the theological task, however, his statement that "theology can be systematic only if it is transcendent" becomes understandable, if still problematic. Proceeding from the methodological stance of "The Size of God," Axel calls for a theology that would address and clarify "the depths and immediacies" of concrete experience, one that would seek "to empower the practice of authentic presence." Such a theology would assist, he says, in the "immersion in life, in the intensification of experience." It would promote a stance of "religious creaturalism."

This conception of the theological task creates its own tensions. Loomer's career—a career that contained its own kind of ambiguity—was, I think it would be fair to say, devoted to a *theoretical* promotion of the *concrete*. Axel's proposal for reshaping the theological task would all but eclipse the important distinction between the theoretical and the concrete. In what way, then, would theology differ from evocative practices such as poetry, the arts, homiletics, or witness? How are we to assess any truth claims that emerge in this connection? Can second-order, reflective *discourse* of any sort ever plausibly assume the whole *existential* burden that Axel and Loomer both charge traditional theologies with evading or distorting?

Constructive answers to these and other problems are not even implicit in Loomer's work. Definitely explicit, however, is Loomer's endorsement of Axel's negative judgment against theodicies.

Religious and intellectual honesty required Loomer to face up to the challenge of Hume's classic statement of the logical trilemma of evil, divine omnipotence, and divine goodness. Like most process theologians, he was willing to modify the notion of omnipotence to mean, not omnicausality in the unilateral sense, but shared power in the relational sense consistent with a metaphysical pluralism. Yet unlike many process theologians, Loomer became wary of any theodicy that was motivated by an apologetic goal (God is not responsible for evil) or maintained by univocal meanings (God's goodness is infinite). It was not clear to him that there are any empirical grounds for a univocal assertion of divine goodness. In the end, quite apart from the question of the coherence of theism, Loomer finally lost interest in all so-called *explanations* of evil. He embraced with utmost seriousness Whitehead's contention that explanations are simply descriptions of the way in which relations are coordinated.[9]

In recent years contemporary intellectual culture in the West has been reshaping itself in increasingly historicist, pragmatic, and antifoundational, postmodernist directions. Empirical theology shares with postmodernism in general a profound skepticism regarding universal and universalizing claims about the powers of reason, progress, science, language, and the self. What Loomer has deplored as a theology of abstractionism, postmodernist critics have castigated as logocentrism and exposed as traces of a transcendental signifier. It may be that the future of Bernard Loomer's unfinished theological agenda is best comprehended in the context of such projects as Derrida's deconstructionism and Mark Taylor's a/theology. Yet Loomer harbored deep doubts about the very enterprise of theology in our time, and could often be heard to mutter, "Can these dry bones be made to live?" As for his own measurement of how close "The Size of God" might come to reality, it is likely that Loomer would answer with the phrase he loved to repeat from William James: "ever not quite."

---

[9]Cf. Alfred North Whitehead, *Process and Reality*, corrected ed., ed. D. R. Griffin and D. W. Sherburne (New York: Free Press, 1978) 153. See also my article, "Some Problems in Process Theodicy," *Religious Studies* 17 (June 1981): 179-97.

INDEX